abduzeedo

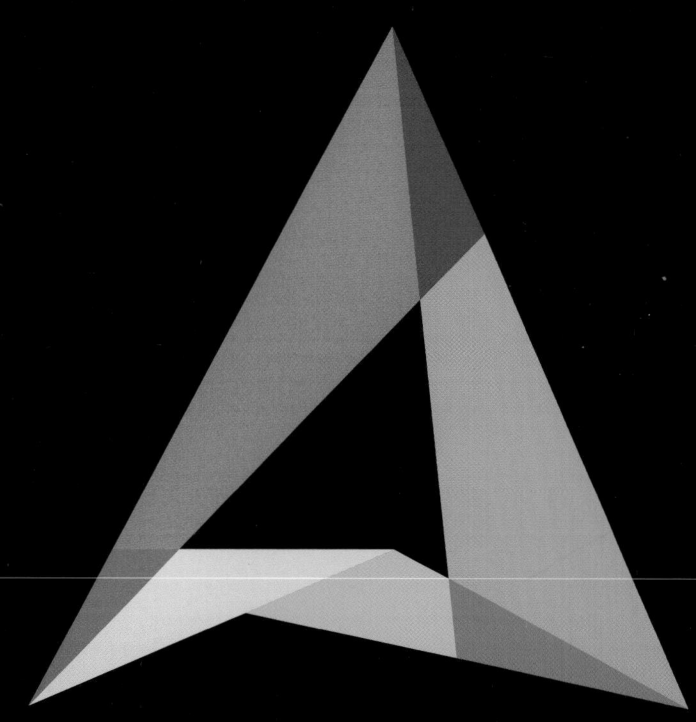

INSPIRATION GUIDE FOR DESIGNERS

Fábio Sasso
and the Abduzeedo Team

ABDUZEEDO INSPIRATION GUIDE FOR DESIGNERS

Fábio Sasso and the Abduzeedo team
New Riders
1249 Eighth Street
Berkeley, CA 94710
510/524-2178
510/524-2221 (fax)
Find us on the Web at: www.newriders.com
To report errors, please send a note to: errata@peachpit.com
New Riders is an imprint of Peachpit, a division of Pearson Education.

Editor: Rebecca Gulick
Production Editor: Tracey Croom
Interior Designers: Fábio Sasso and Andreas F.S. de Danaan
Development Editor: Stephen Nathans-Kelly
Copy Editor: Liz Welch
Proofreader: Patricia Pane
Compositor: Kim Scott, Bumpy Design
Indexer: Rebecca Plunkett
Cover Designer: Fábio Sasso

ISBN-13: 978-0-321-76744-8
ISBN-10: 0-321-76744-6

9 8 7 6 5 4 3 2 1
Printed and bound in the United States of America

Dedication

For my parents, who taught me that everything is possible if done with dedication and love. Thank you from the bottom of my heart. You guys are the best.

Acknowledgments

I clearly remember the moment everything began. It was a hot day in November 2006 in Porto Alegre, Brazil. When my business partner and great friend, Fabiano Meneghetti, and I got back to work after lunch, we saw the door of our office broken in, and then I saw that we had been robbed—all of our laptops, monitors, and backup discs gone. It was terrible, but it was the beginning of a big change in my life.

As crazy as it might sound, if it weren't for the burglars I probably wouldn't have had the opportunity to write this book. And much more than that, I would not have had the chance to meet so many of the talented artists, designers, and people I now call friends. Among them are the amazing friends behind Abduzeedo who helped make this book possible. My thanks to: Fabiano Meneghetti, who was with me from day one; Paulo Gabriel, our first writer; Alexis Papageorgiou, our first international writer from Germany; Paulo Canabarro, a great friend; Gisele Muller, our senior editor and most disciplined contributor; Amanda Macedo, cousin, English teacher, and dharma bum; and François Hoang, a very talented graphic designer and great friend I met in Canada.

I also have to thank Rebecca Gulick for listening to my idea for this book and making it happen for me. Stephen Nathans-Kelly and Liz Welch did an amazing job editing my words. Thanks to Tracey Croom and Kim Scott for their production and layout expertise. And my hat is off to the rest of the Peachpit/New Riders crew for helping to bring this book into reality. I am grateful to have had such pros on my side.

Contents

Introduction

Back in the '90s, when I was just starting my career as graphic designer, I didn't even know such a job title existed. All I knew was that I was creating things like logos and layouts for posters. The Internet was still just starting in my country, Brazil, and our access to information was generally limited to books rather than websites. If you wanted to learn how to use the most popular design applications like Photoshop and Illustrator, the best route was to buy a book about the software and follow it. Even though a great variety of books were available, most of them focused on filters and other technical topics, with little attention paid to art and design principles.

With the Internet came the overflow of information, and soon we had websites and forums to help us in the learning process. With the advent of Web 2.0 came the popularization of blogs and the explosion of users and experts sharing their ideas and knowledge online, which complemented the instruction available through books.

In 2006, I created Abduzeedo (www.abduzeedo.com), a blog dedicated to sharing designs and design knowledge. To be honest, I had never seen a reason to have a blog until that year. My brother had a blog, and he told me I should have one too. I always said that I didn't see any reason for that, probably because I used to worry too much about what to blog about, who would read it, and the possibility that nobody would like my work.

My attitude changed in 2006 when my office was robbed and I lost my computer and my two backup hard disks. I realized the need for offsite backup, and decided that if I was going to back up my work online, I might as well make it publicly available on a site that not only housed my work, but also shared my creative process. So Abduzeedo was born out of the necessity of backing up my files in a way that even if I lost all my hardware again, I would still have all my backups—and so would anyone else who cared to look at them.

Today, after more than four years of operation, Abduzeedo has grown a lot and has become much more than a personal blog. It's evolved into a place to find inspiration and learn about design and design apps. It's also given me the chance to make new friends and meet designers I've always admired. My personal goal was to share new ideas and techniques that I've discovered, as well as things I've learned during my career—especially the ones that I've spent the most time trying to figure out.

In a way, this book is an extension of all the ambitions I've had for the site, a way to gather them in a place where the type of insight and instruction and inspiration I've provided on the site is organized around the key styles and movements that define design and illustration today.

Each chapter is broken down into four sections: Introduction, Gallery, Interview, and Tutorial. In the Introduction sections, I provide some background on each of our major design styles and genres: Abstract Art, Retro, Illustration, Photo Manipulation, Light Effects, Vector Art, and Neosurrealism. These sections are designed to supply a context or a foundation for everything that follows in the chapter.

In the Gallery sections (which share some space with the Intro sections), I've assembled a showcase of some of the most exciting and definitive work being done in each genre today. There you should find plenty of inspiration for your own work as you see how other artists have explored the possibilities inherent to a given style.

With the interviews, I've brought in other voices—just as we do on Abduzeedo—to give you a peek inside the minds of designers and illustrators working in different styles and doing some of the most exciting work in the field today. The interviews will also give you a sense of the arc of their careers, as well as some insight into their creative processes.

Finally, with the tutorial included in each chapter—some written by me and others by guest authors (and fellow designers)—the book will take you step by step through the process of creating an illustration or design that will help you see what you can do in a particular style and how you can achieve it in Photoshop or Illustrator.

In short, I've put together the kind of design book that I wish had been available back in the '90s when I was getting started in graphic design and looking for the guidance and inspiration that I wanted to propel my art and my career forward. As a complement to the wonderful range of resources now available to designers and illustrators available online today, this book provides exactly that sort of assistance for you as you expand your knowledge base and develop your talent and skills.

CHAPTER 1

ABSTRACT ART

By the end of the 19th century, many artists felt a need to create a new kind of art that would reflect the fundamental changes taking place in technology, science, and philosophy. Inspired by Western art that had, since the Renaissance, reproduced an illusion of visible reality, these artists developed a new style known as *abstract art*. Abstract art is a visual language that uses forms, color, and lines to create a composition that serves as a kind of independent art, encompassing almost any visual reference in the world. We can define abstract art in the most basic terms as an exaggeration of something simple.

The first abstract art ever created appeared in 1908 with the emergence of a style called *Cubism*, which originated in the paintings of Pablo Picasso and Georges Braque. Picasso based his first cubist paintings on Paul Cézanne's idea that all depiction of nature can be reduced to three solids: cube, sphere, and cone.

CONSTANT STARTLE,
by Benjamin Low

Three other movements contributed to the abstract style: Romanticism, Impressionism, and Expressionism. But the difference between abstract art and these other forms is the liberties it takes. Paintings in those earlier styles may alter the colors and forms of something real, but they will still allow you to see where the image comes from. At most, these paintings are only partially abstract. Abstract art breaks with this tradition, tracing lines without any reference to anything you can recognize.

In the 1950s and '60s came the resurgence of figurative art, with movements such as Neo-Dada, conceptual art, Neo-Expressionism, video art, and pop art, coming to signify the age of consumerism. The distinction between abstract and figurative art has, over the last 20 years, become less defined than it was when these figurative forms first emerged, leaving all artists with a wider range of ideas from which to draw their work

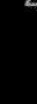

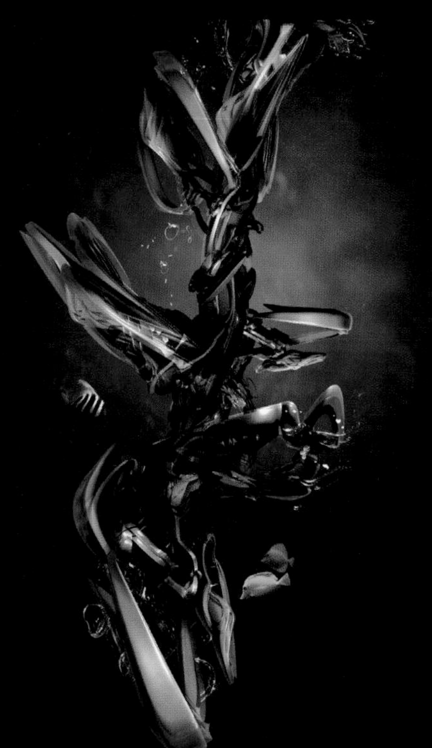

1. *Diego Rodriguez,* **NEEDLES**
2. *El Nombre,* **BREAKTHROUGH**
3. *El Nombre,* **CURIOSITY**
4. *El Nombre,* **ENVY**

1

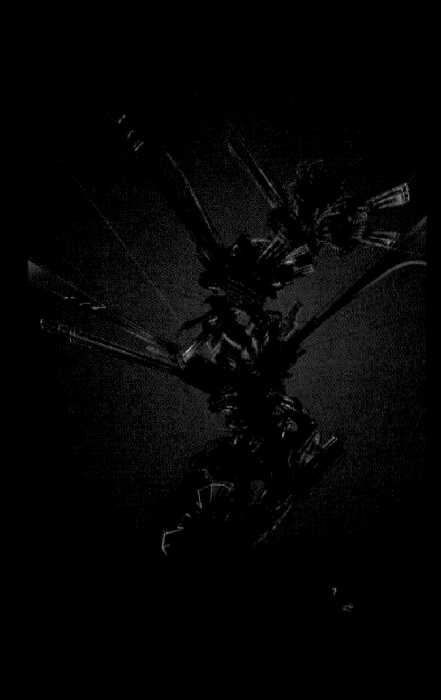

2

3

1. *El Nombre,* FREAK SYSTEM
2. *El Nombre,* HUH
3. *El Nombre,* MELANCHOLY
4. *El Nombre,* IRV2

In his book *Pictures of Nothing*, art historian KIRK VARNEDOE provides an interesting view on the sources and intentions of abstract art:

> Abstract art is propelled by … hope and hunger. It reflects the urge to push toward the limit, to colonize the borderland around the opening onto nothingness, where the land has not been settled, where the new can emerge. That is part of what drives modernity: the urge to regenerate ourselves by bathing in the extreme, for better and for worse. What is remarkable is that abstract art, which was initially advanced by its advocates as a culture of crypto-religious, timeless certainties, associated closely with the new monolithic collectivism in society, should have been reinvented and flourished in the last fifty years as a paradigmatic example of secular diversity, individual initiative, and private vision. It is a prime case of modern Western society's willingness to vest the fate of its communual culture in the play of independent subjectivities, and to accept the permanent uncertainties, pluralities, and never-ending, irresolvable debate that come

4

1. *Fabio Sasso,* FINAL
2. *Evan Bohringer,* A
3. *El Nombre,* TRAIN OF THOUGHT
4. *El Nombre,* TUMBLEDOWN REDUX

1

A typical example of abstract art is a nonrealistic painting that allows you only to imagine the meaning behind the work, rather than spelling it out for you clearly. Today, technology brings us new forms for exploring the abstract. Abstract art now walks alongside digital art, computer art, Internet art, hyperrealism photorealism, minimalism, pop art, graffiti, and other forms of 21st century modern expression.

With these new movements, we start to know new artists, designers who incorporate abstract art into their finished designs and assembled creations. These artists have found ways to mix photos and vectors, retaining the root of abstract art while exploring everything that new computer-based applications provide to help them create a new "digital abstract" art.

2

3

4

2

3

1. *Mart Biemans,* **BEAUTY OF GOLD**
2. *Sergei Vlasov,* **BEYOND THE SEA**
3. *Sergei Vlasov,* **ENVOY**
4. *Mart Biemans,* **I SAID MOVE**

1

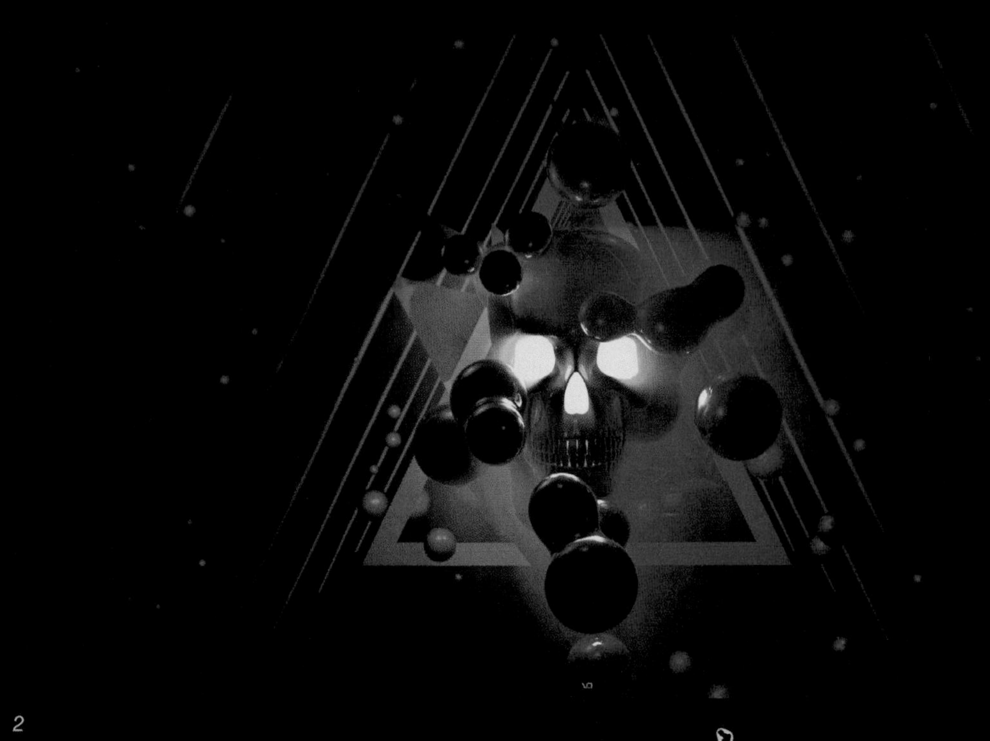
2

1. *Sergei Vlasov,* **FEELINGS INSIDE**
2. *Sergei Vlasov,* **LOOKING**
3. *Sergei Vlasov,* **NEON LIFE**
4. *Olli-pekka Jauhlainen,* **LE CIRQUE DES COULERS**
5. *Sergei Vlasov,* **OLE MEMORIES**

3

4

5

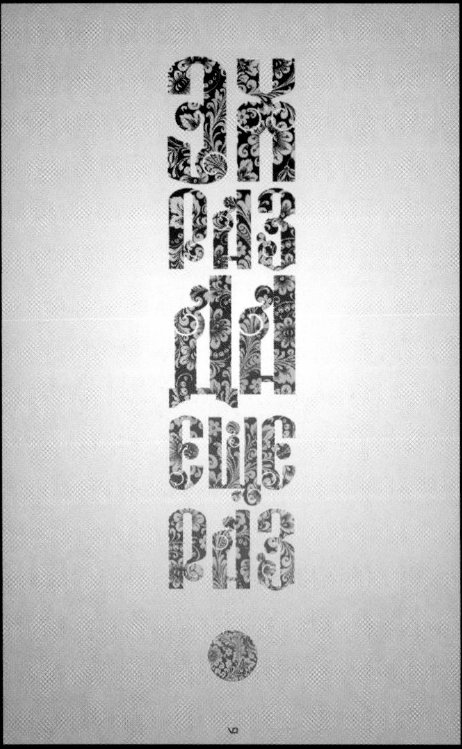

1

2

3

1. *Sergei Vlasov,* SLAVANSK

2. *Sergei Vlasov,* TENDENC

3. *Sergei Vlasov,* XXIV

4. *Felix Ajenjo,* AUTHORITY BLOWING AWAY

5. *Sergei Vlasov,* XXII

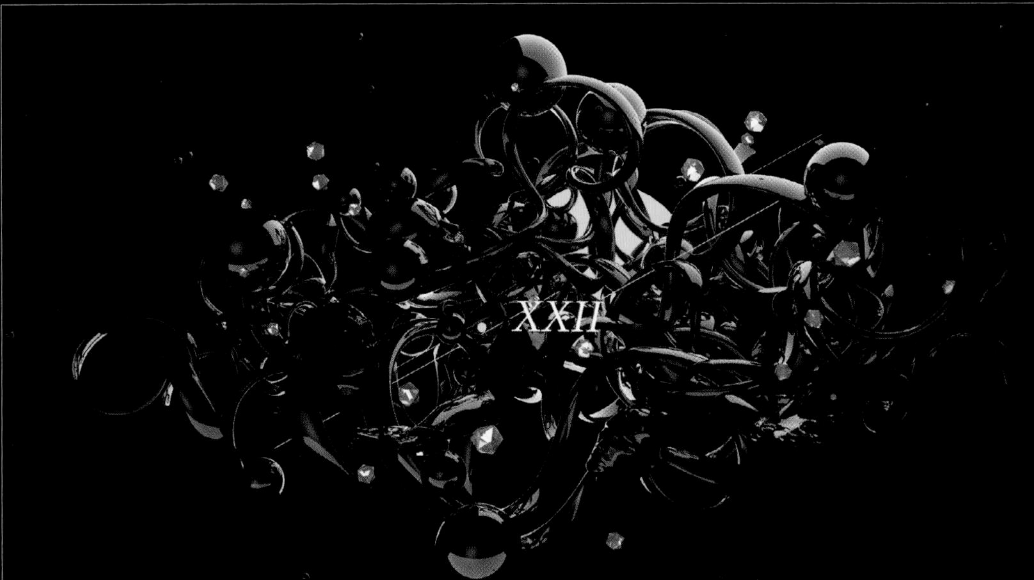

4

XXII

1. *David Mascha,* TRANSIENT 1
2. *David Mascha,* TRANSIENT 2
3. *Pete Harrison (Aeiko),* IN JAPAN

1

SHIPWRECKED
IN JAPAN
津喜谊行
迎西天
harmony in japan

1

1. *Perrtu Murto,* BLACK HOLE
2. *Jeff Huang,* LEVIATHAN
3. *Jeff Huang,* TIMELESS
4. *Jeff Huang,* THE MAMMON MACHINE
5. *Jeff Huang,* GRT

2

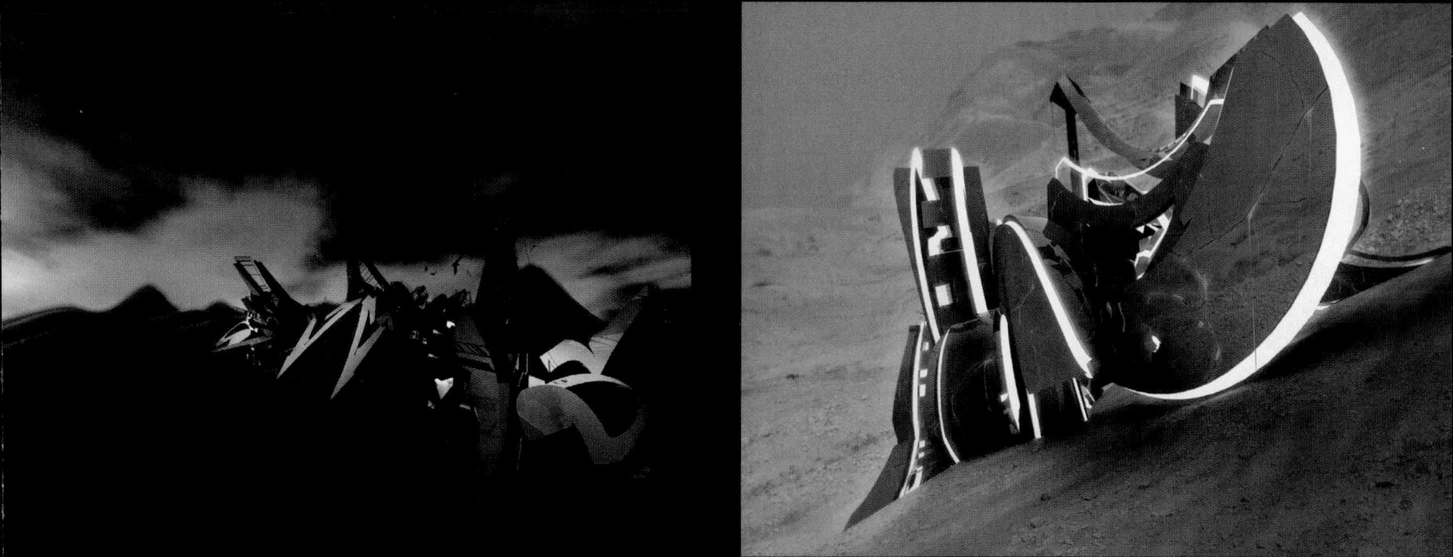

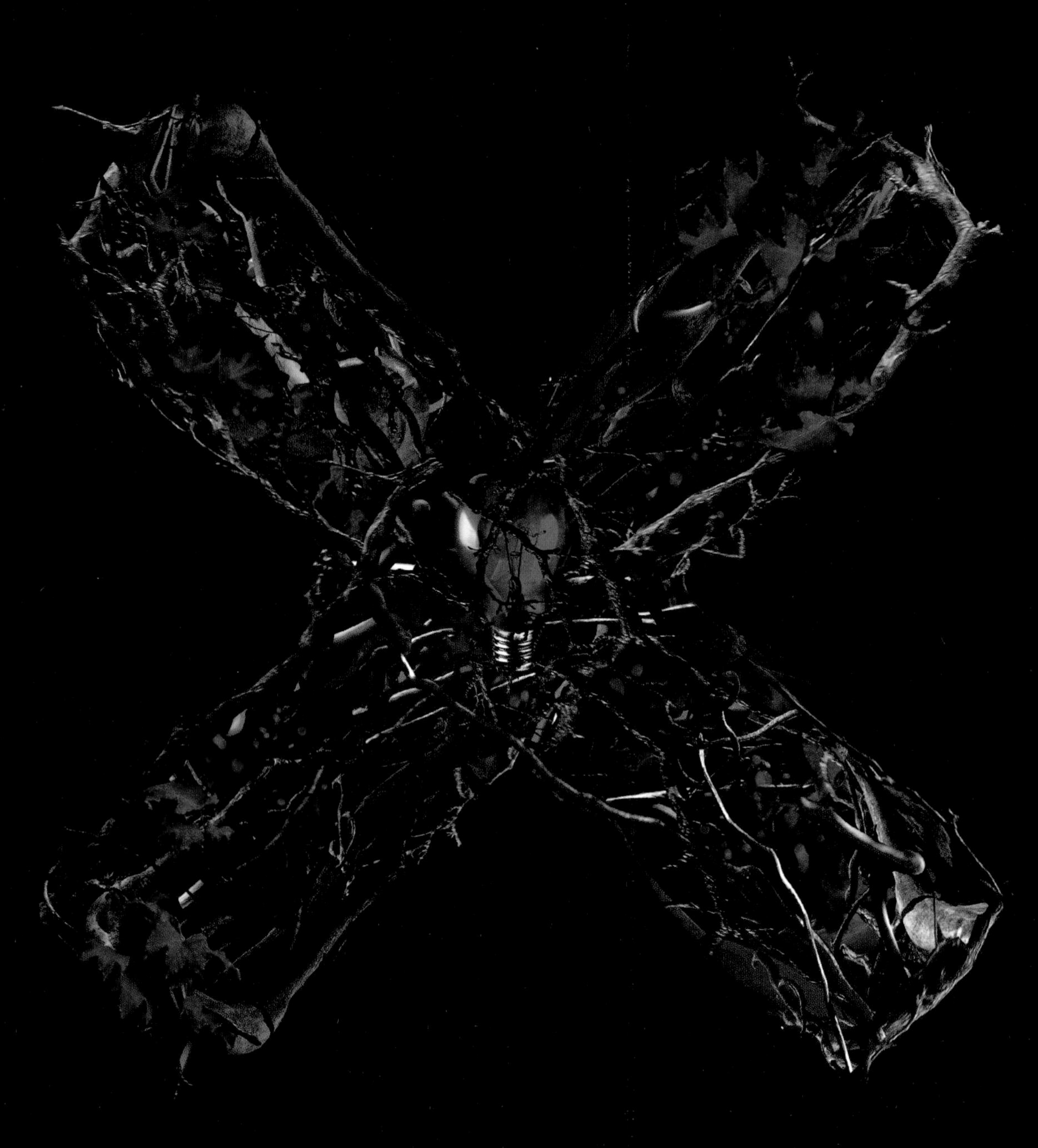

Interview

Justin Maller

Justin Maller, an Australian freelance illustrator and art director now based in Brooklyn, has been creating digital art for over 10 years, and has produced professionally in both a private and studio-based capacity for the last four years.

Justin has produced illustrations and concept art for a wide range of companies and publications worldwide. He is an inner core member of the Keystone Design Union, and also Creative Director of The Depthcore Collective, an international modern art collective established in June 2002.

How did you start your career as digital artist? Did you always know that you wanted to pursue digital art as a career?

My career evolved pretty naturally. It certainly wasn't planned; I went to university to study creative writing and theater. Digital art was my hobby; I was passionate about it, and enjoyed creating and experimenting with it for years before I did my first commercial project. I put up a personal folio to share the work, and was able to show a lot of it in art magazines. In time, I started to attract work, and the results from those jobs attracted more work. Soon I had a full-time freelance career on my hands.

How did you come up with your style, and what made you explore it? What, in your opinion, is your style's defining characteristic?

The work I create now is a long way from the sort of work I started out with. Initially, I was creating primarily abstract stuff using 3D renders. Over time, I started to experiment with incorporating different elements and mediums. In 2006, I hit upon working photography in with my renders, and that was the start of what has probably come to be my signature style. I have had long phases where I worked solely on photographs *sans* renders, but especially in a professional context, I frequently find myself working with the illustrative elements as well.

How would you describe your workflow for your projects?

My process is probably quite comparable to that of a mad scientist: I just get in the lab and go. I don't sketch; I don't plan; I don't even think of ideas. I just start making things. Obviously, if it's a client project, then there are briefs and assets and guidelines involved, so that streamlines the process. But when it comes to personal work, I just start jamming and see what I have eight hours later.

How important is the computer in your creative process?

For my process, it's invaluable. From beginning to end, I use the computer. I was never a talented traditional artist; my visual creativity has always begun and ended with digital software. Without it, I'd have nothing. It used to bother me that I didn't have pencil skills, but over time I've come to realize that I've simply approached art from a different perspective than was previously possible, which is probably why my work is somewhat distinctive.

Could you list some artists or designers that you admire, in terms of style, and describe why you hold them in such high regard?

A lot of the folks in Depthcore are producing work that I admire greatly. Nik Ainley has always been at the very forefront of the digital art world; no matter how far it progresses, he is always a step ahead in terms of originality and attention to detail—the two things I hold in the highest regard.

Jon Foerster is another chip off this block, but I hold him in even greater esteem because of his dogged pursuit of the abstract. He has recently started using photographic elements in his work, but his powerful compositions are still dominated by intricate and beautiful, organic, abstract forms. Making a cohesive and interesting piece just out of renders in this day and age is exceedingly difficult, but he makes it look easy.

Tell us about some of your own works that you're proudest of and why they're so important for you.

My recent piece for Kobe Bryant (page 26) is something I am very proud of. I put a lot of work and development into that piece, expanding on his existing brand concepts and personality traits to create a piece that I think will stand up as a pretty fresh take on the sports art genre for some time. I am a huge fan of basketball, and creating the piece was a real pleasure for me; I think the end result shows just how much fun I had with it.

Apart from the money it brings in, what type of satisfaction do you get from your work? And how much does this matter in your life?

I get a wonderful feeling of satisfaction when I get a head of steam and am really making progress on a piece. I look at what's in front of me, remember how it started, and just take pride in the time and effort I put into the creative process. It's a wonderful release, and I'm fortunate that I am able to get that from a lot of my client projects as well as from my own personal work.

What advice do you have for those who are starting out their careers? What kind of references are important for those who want to work with the type of style you have?

I think the most important thing for anyone interested in pursuing a creative career is to just be honest with yourself throughout, and be aware of some of the realities that come along with having your passion as your career. Number one: It has to be your passion. Ain't no such thing as halfway, crooks. You have to have a real love for what you do, and—to be perfectly honest—a real talent.

However, more important than talent is a good work ethic; no one opened Photoshop and was amazing in it in a week. Everyone who is on top of the game at the moment is there because they put in the work; they did 12-hour days for weeks on end, just fiddling and experimenting for no pay. There are dues to be paid, lessons to be learned. A lot of them are the kind of lessons that schools can't teach you. Be aware that this is a long journey, and it takes a lot of passion and commitment to come out of it with a career.

Tutorial

Abstract Art

In this tutorial, you'll learn how to design abstract art digitally, creating an image that's not bound by reality or any visible connection to its source.

Step 1

To begin, open a Photoshop document using the image of this model (**1**). This image came from the website StockFresh.com, a great site for beautiful images at an affordable price. To download this image, go to http://stockfresh.com/image/706244/pretty-blond-lady.

Step 2

At the bottom of the Layers panel, click the "Create a new fill or adjustment layer" icon and choose Hue/Saturation.

Change the Saturation value to 20. Doing so creates a gray color overlay with the tone of the model's body (**2**).

Step 3

Create a new layer, set the background layer to a dark gray (#242424), and put it underneath the layer of the model.

Now you'll need to extract the background of the model. Choose Tools > Quick Selection Tool and select all the main elements all around the model to extract them. After selecting and clearing the background, you can always go back and work more on the hair or the body masking using the Refine Mask tool (Select > Refine Mask).

When your mask is complete, make the model's hair white by clicking the "Create a new fill or adjustment layer" icon at the bottom of the Layers panel. Choose Desaturate and then mask the hair with a Layer mask (**3**).

1

2

3

Step 4

Create a new layer and put it underneath the layer of the model. Select the Gradient tool and choose Radial Gradient with the preset of Foreground to Transparent. Choose a light gray (#7c7c7c) for the foreground and a dark gray (#242424) for the transparency.

Apply the Gradient tool to wherever you think it would be cool to locate the source of light around the model. Then duplicate the same layer to give a more powerful light effect to the background (**4**).

Step 5

Select the Ellipse tool (U) and make a white (#ffffff) circle. Blend the layer to create an overlay using the Blending options of the Layers panel (**5**).

Duplicate the white circle layer, and use Edit > Transform > Scale to transform it to a smaller size. Put the white circle layer on the model's left size close to her neck and armpit, as shown in the previous image.

Step 6

Now we need to add another image to the composition. We need a smashed glass, which you can download from http://creativeoverflow.net/wp-content/uploads/2010/02/Smashed-Glass.jpg.

Place the smashed glass right in front of the model, and make sure that the image is perfectly in the middle. Then simply blend it to screen using the Blending options of the Layers panel (**6**).

4

5

6

Step 7

The image could use some more depth around the broken glass in the upper-right corner of the model. To address this, duplicate the broken glass layer, select Edit > Transform > Rotate, and rotate the layer 180 degrees. After rotating the new broken glass layer, add a Layer mask from the bottom of the Layers panel (**7**).

Step 8

Take the same broken glass layer and duplicate it again. To create a crisper effect, select the new layer, and choose Edit > Transform > Scale to scale it as shown; then place it in the middle of the model, as shown (**8**).

Step 9

The source point of this artwork was the model's heart, so we need to add some lighting. To do so, we'll add a flare image that you can download at www.shutterstock.com/pic-49249912-stock-photo-lens-flare-artistic-effect-isolated-on-black-background.html.

Paste the flare image in the middle. Then blend it to screen using the Blending options of the Layers panel (**9**).

Step 10

Create a new layer. Select the Pen tool (P), and trace a shape that would represent the glass reflection. Then choose Layer > Rasterize > Shape to rasterize this new glass reflection layer.

Create another layer and repeat this process for the glass reflection from the right (**10**).

Step 11

This next step is a bit tricky to describe, but it's easy to accomplish. Go into the Layers panel and flatten the image, but don't save your artwork—you'll lose all the layers! Using the Rectangle Marquee tool (M), select the model's face. Then copy your selection using Edit > Copy.

Now unflatten your artwork and save. When you're done saving, select the left glass reflection from step 10 and paste your selection into the layer by selecting Edit > Paste Special > Paste Into. Arrange the composition just the way you like. Create a reflection using Edit > Transform > Flip Horizontal, and apply a little rotation by selecting Edit > Transform > Rotate (**11**).

Step 12

In this step, you'll create the background elements of the broken glass. You'll work with a broken glass stock brush that you can download at http://imgs.abduzeedo.com/files/book/brokenglass_brushsample.jpg.

Create a new layer, select the Brush tool, choose dark gray (#242424) for the background color, and select the brush. Play around with the brush until you get an effect you like, and blend the layer to overlay using the Blending options in the Layers panel.

To finish this step, add a Radial Blur effect for the edges by selecting Filter > Blur > Radial Blur. Set the amount to 1 for the best spin (**12**). Doing so will add a little motion feel to the edges of the brush.

10

11

12

Step 13

Now you need to download a fractal image to add another element to the composition. Go to http://greentunic.deviantart.com/gallery/?offset=24#/d1jcykh and download the image, and add it to the project. Then blend the fractal-image layer to screen to extract the black background color, and place it as if the elements of this layer were part of the dress (**13**). Repeat the same process until you're satisfied with the result.

Step 14

Use the same process described in step 13 for the fractal image, but with a different color. Again, place the source image and play with the Blending options until you're satisfied with the result (**14**).

Conclusion

Finally, you can add little touches to customize this artwork in your desired style. Welcome to the world of abstract art!

13

14

GTFO

CHAPTER 2

RETRO ART

The word *retro*—which derives from the Latin prefix *retro*, meaning "backwards" or "in past times"—typically refers to a mode, trend, or style that is identified with a different time in the recent past but that still enjoys our attention and appreciation. Our attraction to retro styles has always been strong, bringing to mind outdated trends, fashion, products, culture, and the like and transforming them into something cool again. In 2011, retro styles currently in vogue tend to come from the '70s and '80s, and this is how it usually works: We revive a trend from 20–40 years ago and put it back into circulation. We may describe these retro styles or trends as "vintage" or "old school," but the meaning is essentially the same. From color schemes to typography, from clothes to vinyl records, from Atari to *Tron* (the original from 1982, that is), many things that used to be popular a while back are now making a comeback in art, cars, TV, fashion, music, and culture.

OFFF 2011,
by Pete Harrison (Aeiko)

In her insightful book *Retro: The Culture of Revival*, ELIZABETH E. GUFFEY had this to say about our cultural affinity for the fashionably old and outmoded:

As Voltaire noted, history does not change, but what we want from it does. "Retro" carries a pervasive, if somewhat imprecise meaning: gradually creeping into daily usage over the past thirty years, there have been few attempts to define it. Used to describe cultural predisposition and personal taste, technological obsolescence, and mid-century style, "retro's" neologism rolls off the tongue with an ease that transcends slang.

We can easily agree with Guffey and say that the term retro has become the buzzword for describing some trends. We can also agree that at times we overuse the term, applying it to everything that is not totally new to recast it as something old-fashioned or antique. This frenzy of enthusiasm for reviving styles derives from a nostalgic impulse to rescue designs that were cool a while back in the hope that they might become cool again. It's a feeling of admiration for the past, a revivalism where the present reuses the past.

1

2

3

4

5

1. *Alex Varanese,* ALT 197 MOBILEVOXX ABSTRACT
2. *Alex Varanese,* ALT 1977 LAPTRON 64 ABSTRACT
3. *Alex Varanese,* ALT 1977 LAPTRON 64 AD
4. *Alex Varanese,* ALT 1977 MICROCADE 3000 ABSTRACT
5. *Alex Varanese,* ALT 1977 MICROCADE 3000 STUDY
6. *Alex Varanese,* ALT 1977 LOGO

6

1

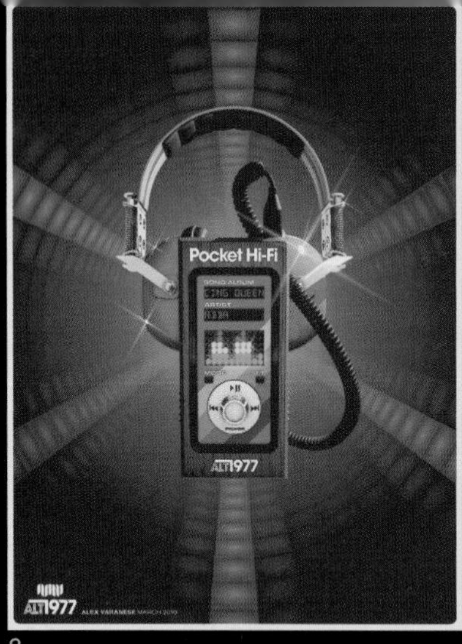

2

3

1. *Alex Varanese,* ALT 1977 MOBILEBVOXX AD
2. *Alex Varanese,* ALT 1977 POCKET HI-FI ABSTRACT
3. *Alex Varanese,* ALT 1977 POCKET HI-FI AD
4. *Alex Varanese,* BAROQUEN 0
5. *Alex Varanese,* BAROQUEN 2
6. *Alex Varanese,* THE METRO ENCAPSULATION
7. *Alex Varanese,* THE METRO INTERVIEW
8. *Alex Varanese,* TYPEFACE DECODER

Retro in Design

"Retro" styles appear in current designs from all fields we can imagine, from digital to print and web design; designers of all stripes seem to love using retro elements. Whether it's bright colors, bold designs, groovy letters, lava lamps, or old-school combinations of shapes and images, angles, or curves, everything that was a hit in the past is back in play today.

Even though technology is always evolving and opening up new and previously unexplored design possibilities, its forward push doesn't stop designers from embracing styles popular in past decades with works based on pure nostalgia. Designers still love and get inspired by outmoded styles such as high-waist jeans, simple yet bold graphics, and big hairstyles. Retro-style design has always been around, but in the past few years it has simply exploded. Several prominent designers are using famous old-school elements to give a nostalgic feeling to their pieces. It's nice to see design elements from the past being reused in the middle of these times of technological revolution.

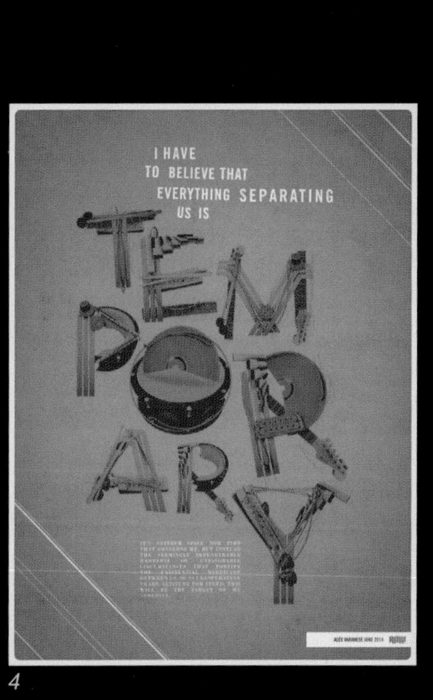
I HAVE
TO BELIEVE THAT
EVERYTHING SEPARATING
US IS
TEMPORARY

4

ICE
SLEET
SNOW
ALEX VARANESE JUNE 2010

5

6

7

ISLANDS
BORDERING NOWHERE AND SEPARATING NOTHING

8

In their book *New Retro: Classic Graphics, Today's Designs*, BRENDA DERMODY and TERESA BREATHNACH perfectly capture this trend in its current context:

> Reinterpreting the past—the greatest form of creative flattery—never goes out of fashion. In the midst of today's technologically driven design, there has been a return to the comfort of familiar imagery and typography, particularly from the twentieth century.

This description is totally accurate for today's digital designers: We use typography and colors that remind us of past times, good times, or simply to rescue a past that we feel connected to.

1

2

3

4

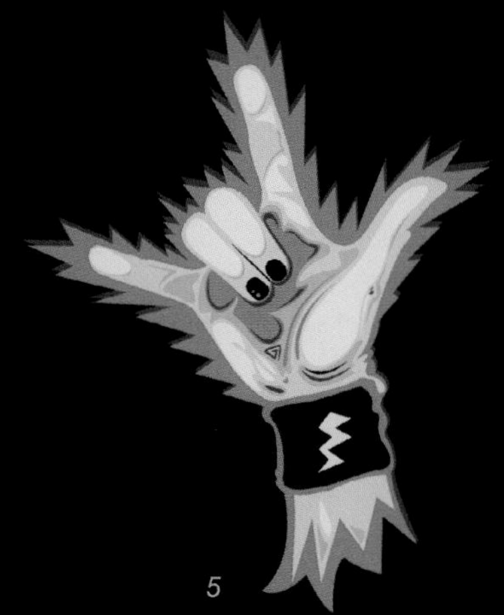

5

6

1. *Fabio Sasso,* '80S INSPIRATION
2. *Fabio Sasso,* FLOWER
3. *Fabio Sasso,* HALFTONE
4. *Genaro De Sia Coppola,* CORRUPTED
5. *Genaro De Sia Coppola,* ILU
6. *Genaro De Sia Coppola,* PUNKIT

Interview

James White

James White is a graphic designer and digital artist from Halifax, Nova Scotia, Canada. He is the founder of SignalNoise Studio (www.signalnoise.com), which was recently acquired by Viacom. Over the last 11 years, James has worked on an array of personal art projects and has worked with such clients as Toyota, Nike, Google, VH1, Armada Skis, and *Wired Magazine*, and has been featured in *Computer Arts, Computer Arts Projects*, and *Advanced Photoshop* magazines. He has become quite popular because of his super-cool retro style mixed with some beautiful light effects. James has some very insightful thoughts about creativity and the creative process.

How did you start your career as a digital artist and designer? Did you always know that you wanted to be an artist?

I have been drawing ever since I could hold a pencil at the age of 4, constantly getting in trouble for doodling in class while in school. When I was in grade 12, my guidance counselor gave me a brochure outlining all the courses at the Nova Scotia Community College (NSCC) in my hometown of Truro. While going through it, I noticed they offered a course in graphic design. Up until that point, it had never occurred to me that I could do something creative as a career. I applied immediately, and was accepted a few weeks later in 1995.

After a year of graphic design, I was accepted into another course at the NSCC called Interactive Technology, which taught me the technology side of things, such as CD-ROM, video editing, sound recording, and animation. Most importantly, it taught me how to construct websites. Upon graduation in 1998, I was scooped up in the web boom and proceeded to work professionally in the industry for 10 years.

I didn't really know what graphic design was until I read the description in that NSCC brochure when I was 18. I had been drawing just because I enjoyed doing it with no greater motive in mind. This kind of blind enjoyment still resonates in my personal art to this day: I do it because I love it.

How did you come up with your style, and what made you explore it further?

My artistic journey into style and expression is still evolving to this day. I spent the majority of my 20s doing all kinds of personal artwork such as comic book illustration, children's book illustration, sculpting, painting, flyer design, 3D, Flash animation—pretty much anything I had an interest in. Even though I had no real direction in mind, inadvertently I got a lot of experience in different areas just by spending years trying different things.

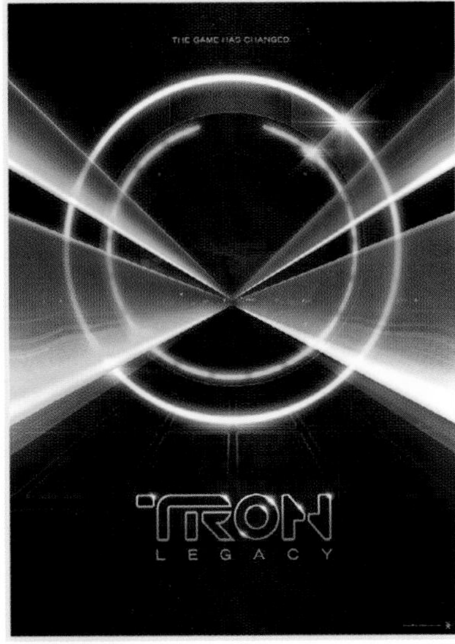

I spent my evenings and weekends constantly working on stuff.

Eventually, I got tired of the random nature of my work going in all directions, and decided to start a blog to give myself a more linear direction to follow. It was a perfect medium because I could work on something, upload it, and then talk about its creation and the inspiration behind it.

After a little while of doing digital paintings of skulls and things, I made a conscious decision to look to my childhood for inspiration. As a typical kid growing up in the '80s, I was into *Star Wars*, *Transformers*, and *The A-Team*. A staple in all of these was studio and network logo animations from that time. I remember seeing the brightly colored NBC peacock, the CBS eye, and that amazing CBS Special Presentation promo (YouTube it!), and I wanted to incorporate that aesthetic into my work. I never lost touch with all of these visuals from my childhood, and with the rise of YouTube, I had them instantly at my fingertips once again. It's almost time-traveling.

How would you describe your workflow for your projects? How important is the computer in your creative process?

Every project I do, and every piece I create starts with the sketchbook. I normally gather whatever references or inspiration I need, then get away from the computer with my sketchbook to start doodling rough ideas of the direction I would like to move in. Under most circumstances, I have a vague idea in my head of what I want to achieve, but it's not until I rough out the thumbnails on paper that the concept really starts to take shape. Sometimes, I do up to 20 or 30 thumbnails before I get

something I'm happy with. Only then will I move to the computer.

Before I start building the design, I create a digital sketch in Adobe Illustrator. This is an important part of my process, as it enables me to create a quick color-and-composition study before building the final design. In Illustrator I can easily slide around the elements to see what works and what doesn't, which sometimes yields new ideas and results. I will even take these vectors into Photoshop to throw some effects on top to get a sense of what the final design might look like.

After I'm comfortable with the vector study, I start building the real elements in Illustrator (if needed), then put everything together in Photoshop for the final high-res design. When all of my vector elements are in place, I'll lay in any effects, textures, and color treatments I need. When I build the design in Photoshop, I always leave myself open to try new things along the way, in hopes of stumbling across that happy mistake. The computer is a wonderful tool, but it's easy to make a design look sterile and uninteresting if you use a computer exclusively. If you treat your design like paint and do things off the beaten path, you might be surprised by the outcome.

Can you list some artists and designers you admire?

Josef Muller-Brockmann, Paul Rand, Saul Bass, Dave McKean, Mike Mignola, Shepard Fairey, Scott Hansen, Drew Struzan, Bob Peak, Joshua Davis, Ralph McQuarrie, and Chuck Anderson.

What advice do you have for those who are just starting their careers?

If you're in school, don't do only what your instructor tells you to do. Use what you learn during class to enhance and build your own projects. The more things you make, the better you will know your tools, and the faster you'll grow a unique portfolio. Once you're out of school, don't ever think that you need an employer or a client in order to make things. If you have free time, create personal projects and start seeing them through until completion. Your personal projects are 100 percent personal expression where you make your own rules. Start early, start now.

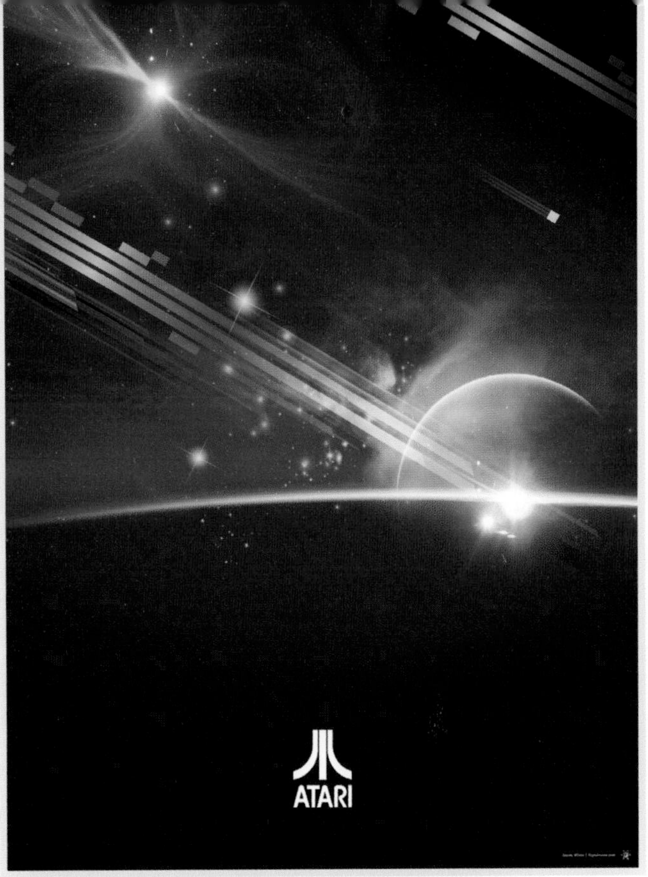

Which part of the creative process do you like the most: before, when you have only the idea and a vision of what it's going to be like; during, the part where you're transforming your idea into your creation; or after, when the work is done and you're looking at the final piece?

Definitely during. When I have an initial idea in my head, it's still difficult for me to envision exactly how the concept will translate to real life. I might have one idea, but along with that come 50 questions that need answering. It's exciting, yet intimidating. Once a piece is finished, it's an amazing rush to see the work printed and hanging on a wall. I love seeing my work come off the screen and onto a poster. However, the best part of my process is actually doing the work. I love the ups and downs a design goes through as I work on it, when I get annoyed that it's not looking good and uplifted when it's going better than expected. It's problem-solving every step of the way, and I also learn a lot about my process as I rip through it.

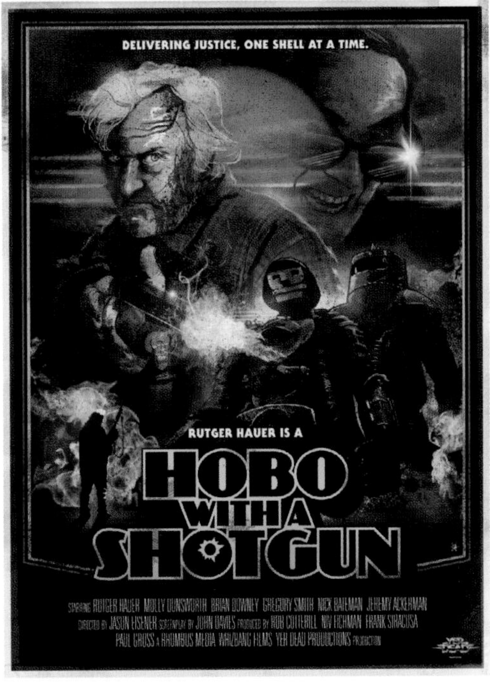

Apart from the money you make, what type of satisfaction do you get from your work?

I love creating. As I said earlier, I've been drawing my entire life so I'm just used to making cool stuff for fun. Clients, employment, profits, and all that stuff are a necessary by-product of what I enjoy doing on my own time. It's that simple. Getting paid is nice, but nothing can beat the feeling of accomplishing something on your own, whether it's launching a line of T-shirts or staying up all night to finish that poster design. Art is who I am, and who I will always be.

What kinds of reference points are important for those who want to work with a retro style?

I always urge people wanting to design things from the past to look at their own childhood for inspiration. Since I grew up in the late '70s and early '80s, this is the era that is forged into my history and something I love building upon. Always do what makes you happy, not just what other people are doing.

But that being said, there are elements of the past that are very potent in the design cues I use in my work. Researching television network animations from the '70s is a huge inspiration as they are packed full of bright colors and vintage animation, while having a certain roughness due to age and film quality. Also look into album covers from the '80s, namely from the hard rock and metal genre. They were big into metal type and lightning, which are elements I love using in my work.

What, in your opinion, is the defining characteristic of your style?

Fun! I never take what I do too seriously, or speak about it as if it were some high form of design. It's a snapshot of me having a great time. I create things that I thought were cool when I was 7 years old, and that really hasn't changed. I could talk about process, effects, and colors, but the most important thing is to have fun and create something from your heart.

James White | Signalnoise.com

ABDUZEEDO

Tutorial

Retro Poster in Illustrator and Photoshop

Creating vintage/retro effects has become quite popular in today's design and illustration worlds. We can see lots of examples of retro-style work on sites such as Dribbble.com. There are quite a few ways to add a retro look to your work; however, one thing you will always have to do when creating retro designs is to play with textures.

In this tutorial, I'll show you how to create a retro poster starting with some sketches, then going to Illustrator to build them digitally, and finally applying textures and effects in Photoshop to give them an unmistakable retro look.

Step 1

Whenever I start a new project, the first thing I do is sketch some ideas. I don't draw particularly well, but even with my limited sketching skills, I find that starting with a pencil sketch is the easiest way to begin to realize my ideas. The idea behind the image we'll work with in this tutorial was to create something inspired by Robert Indiana's *Love* artwork, but in a much more futuristic approach. Instead of using "LOVE," in this tutorial we'll play with the letters "ABDZ" (**1**).

Step 2

Once I'd completed my sketches and had a clear idea of what I wanted to do, I went to Illustrator and started creating the image. When you have your own preliminary sketches done, use the Pen Tool (P) to start drawing the A, which is basically a triangle (**2**). Then invert it using the Transform tool to create part of the Z. Then, with more lines, use the Pen Tool to draw the D and the B.

1

2

3

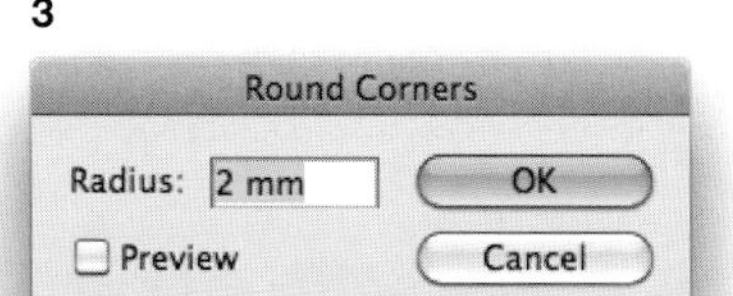

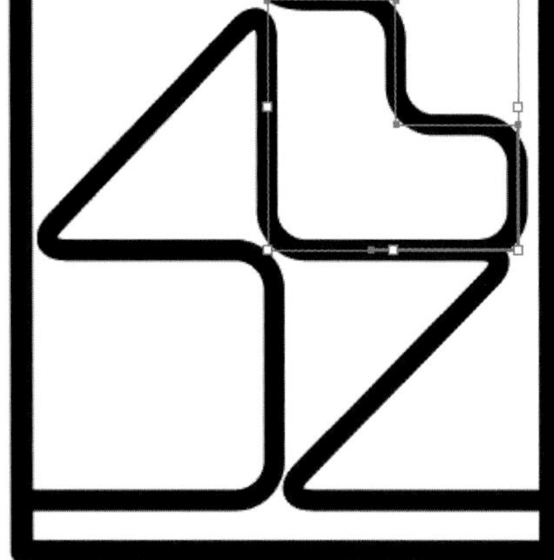

Step 3

After you've drawn a nice set of lines, apply Illustrator's Round Corners filter. You'll note that I made some adjustments in order to make the characters more readable, especially in the spacing between the A and D, the Z and D, and the B and A (**3**).

Step 4

At this point, the ABDZ shape is pretty much done. Next, create a rectangle and fill it with a light brown (#A48A7B). Then use the Pen tool (P), to create a shape to the right of the B and Z and fill it up with yellow (#F7D21E0) to differentiate it from the brown area (**4**). Then do the same for the A, B, and D but fill it with a light blue (#A1C4E9).

Step 5

Now we're ready to move the project into Photoshop. Copy the vectors from Illustrator and paste them into Photoshop as Smart Objects (**5**).

4

5

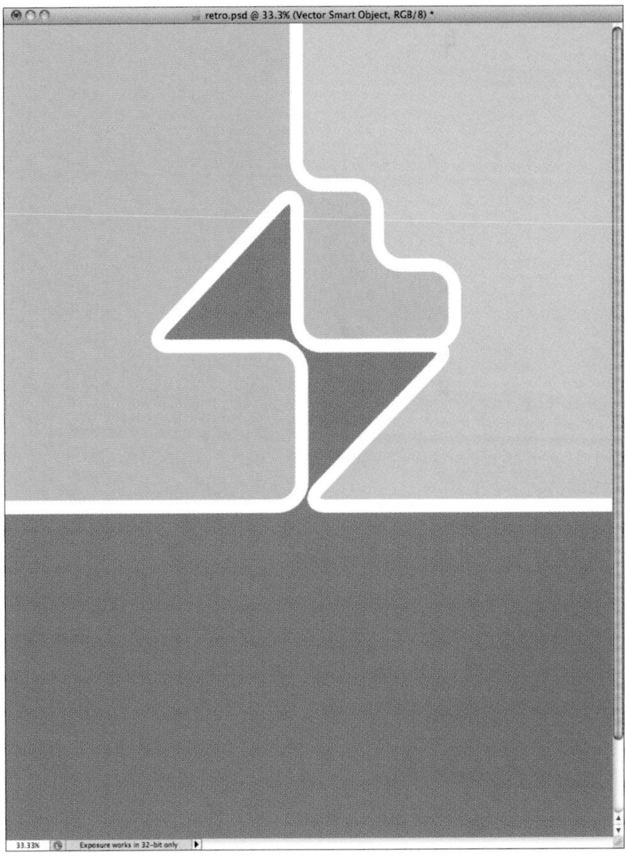

Step 6

Choose Filter > Brush Strokes > Spatter. Enter *1* for Spray Radius and *1* for Smoothness (**6**).

Step 7

To give the image the vintage look we're going for, let's import an old paper texture (**7**). The one I am using comes Shutterstock, and you can find it at www.shutterstock.com/pic-35221027/stock-photo-old-paper.html.

6

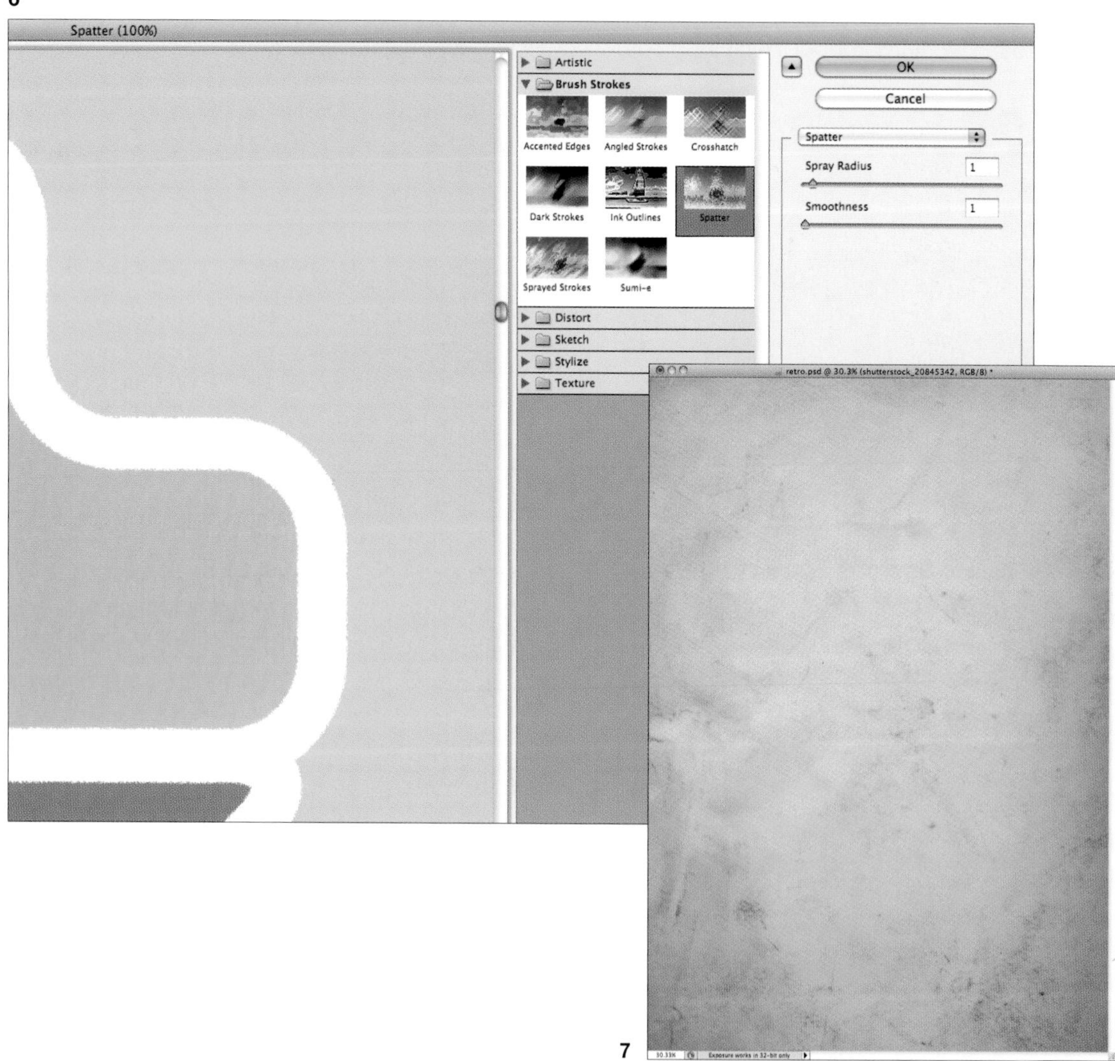

7

Step 8

Change the Blend Mode of the old paper texture to Multiply (**8**).

Step 9

Now it's time to personalize the composition. In my version, I selected the Text tool and added *Abduzeedo* at the bottom, using BlairMdITC as the font (**9**).

Next, select all layers and duplicate them. Select the duplicated layers and merge them into a layer. You can do that with the keyboard shortcut Command (Mac)/Control (PC)+Alt+Shift+E.

Step 10

Choose Filter > Pixelate > Color Halftone (**10**). Use the default options.

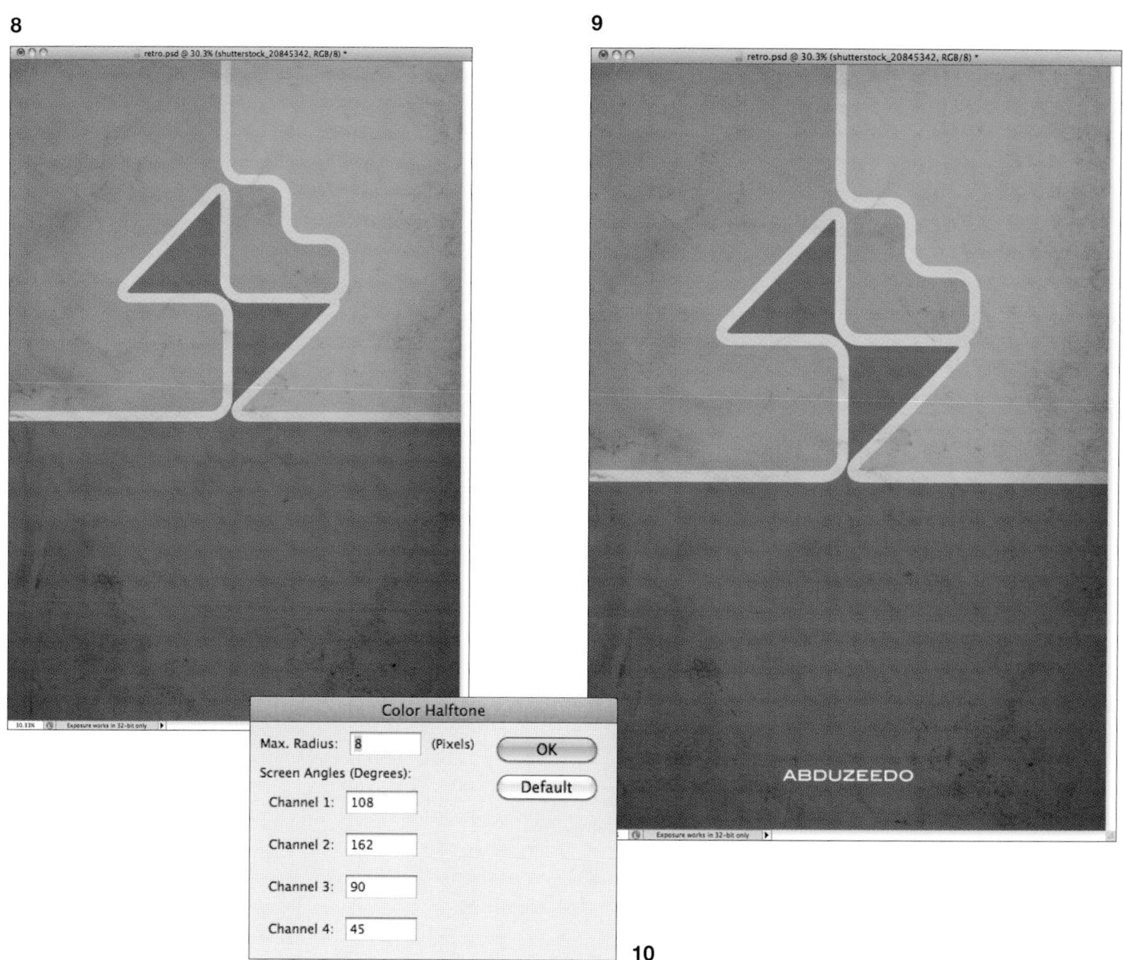

Step 11

Select the layer with the Color Halftone, and change its Blend Mode to Multiply and its Opacity to 30%. The purpose of this layer is to add some texture to the image, as if it was really printed (**11**).

Step 12

Duplicate all the layers again and merge the duplicated layers into a single layer (**12**).

11

12

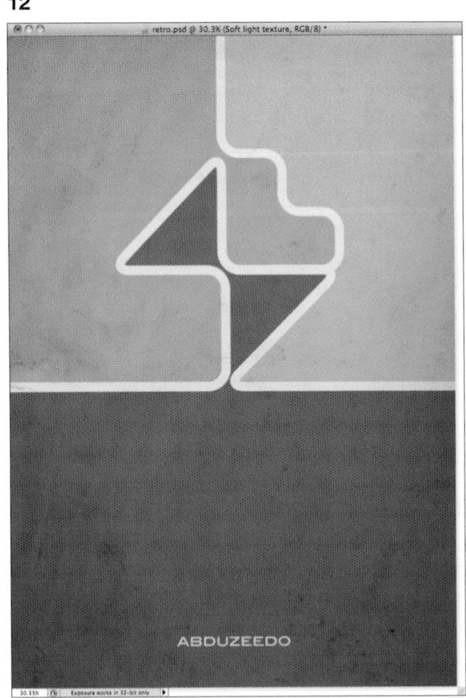

Step 13

With the merged layer selected, choose Filter > Brush Strokes > Crosshatch. Select 9 for the Stroke Length, 6 for the Sharpness, and 1 for the Strength. Then change the Blend Mode of this layer to Soft Light (**13**). Finally, duplicate this layer to make the colors more vivid.

Step 14

Choose Layer > New Adjustment Layer > Hue and Saturation. Select -5 for Hue and -12 for Saturation, but keep Lightness set at the default 0 (**14**). Also make sure that the adjustment layer is on top of all the other layers.

Conclusion

To give a nice retro/vintage look to your designs you must add some textures; textures are an essential component of any retro effect. Sometimes a halftone mixed with some washed colors is the way to go; at other times you'll add some noise to the layer mask, or use brushes to create new textures. Another good tip is to always keep some old paper textures on hand that you can add on top of the layers with Blend Modes like Multiply—that will really do the job.

Once again, it's all about playing with the tools and trying to understand how things work in real life, and then trying to reproduce that on a computer. For coming up with new ideas, however, there's nothing like pencil and paper.

13

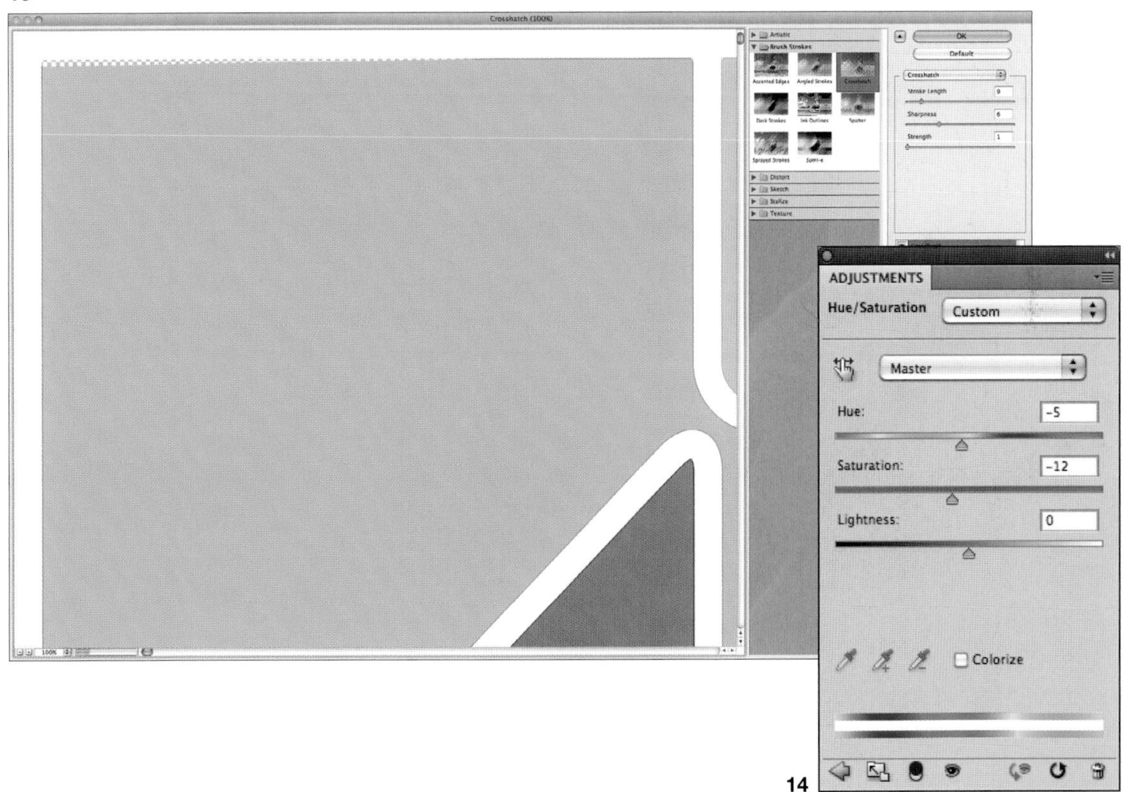

14

CHAPTER 3

ILLUSTRATION

An *illustration* is a pictorial image used to complete, explain, or add information; it can also serve to synthesize or simply decorate a text. Although the term illustration most often refers to drawings, paintings, or collages, a photograph is another type of illustration that may serve these purposes when accompanying a body of text. Furthermore, an illustration is one of the most important elements of graphic design.

Illustrations have been a part of human culture since our ancestors lived in caves. It is in caves that we've found the oldest kind of illustrations: petroglyphs, or rough drawings made in stone, depicting the everyday lives of the people who created them.

DESTROY,
by Adrian Romero

The ancient Egyptians created the oldest known illustrated publication. Titled *The Book of Dead*, it consists of rituals, spells, and procedures intended to help a dead person along the journey to the afterlife.

Beginning near the end of the Roman Empire and the early Christian era, and continuing until the advent of printed books around 1450, monks and other artists cloistered in scriptoria produced richly illustrated and adorned books called *illuminated manuscripts*.

The glitter of the gold pages that often adorned these manuscripts gave the impression that the pages were literally illuminated. The artists and illustrators responsible for the beautification of the pages were known as *illuminators*.

1. *Aiven Media,* OVERDOSE
2. *Carlos Lerma,* BRAINS
3. *Carlos Lerma,* CHIKITA VIOLENTA
4. *Carlos Lerma,* LADY JUSTICE

1

2

CHIKITA
VIOLENTA
+
La Sonrisa
Vertical
Deck B
arts&crafts méxico
BLACK
BOX
feb
25
9:00 pm
$70
Polën®

3

4

Few of these adorned books remain in complete form (save for rare exceptions like *The Book of Kells* housed at Trinity College, Dublin), but the remaining fragments show sequential illustrations much like modern comic books.

Currently, we tend to regard illustrations as pictorial elements that transcend their traditional role. In most cases, illustrations are considered independent content. This trend is especially evident when we consider the role of infography in current publications. With the evolution of pictorial language, it is becoming increasingly difficult to determine the boundaries of content shown in graphic design.

1

2

- *Carlos Lerma,* **LESSON**
- *Carlos Lerma,* **LOS OLVIDADOS**
- *Carlos Lerma,* **ONE AM RADIO (1)**
- *Carlos Lerma,* **ONE AM RADIO (2)**
- *Carlos Lerma,* **PETITS PLAISIRS**
- *Carlos Lerma,* **SOUL INDIE GO**

3

4

1

2

1. *Genaro De Sia Coppola,* **NIGHTLIFE**
2. *Genaro De Sia Coppola,* **LIFE**
3. *Genaro De Sia Coppola,* **STORMY WEATHER**
4. *Genaro De Sia Coppola,* **GUITAR GIRL**
5. *Genaro De Sia Coppola,* **ROLLERGIRL**
6. *Genaro De Sia Coppola,* **SING A SONG**

4

5

6

2

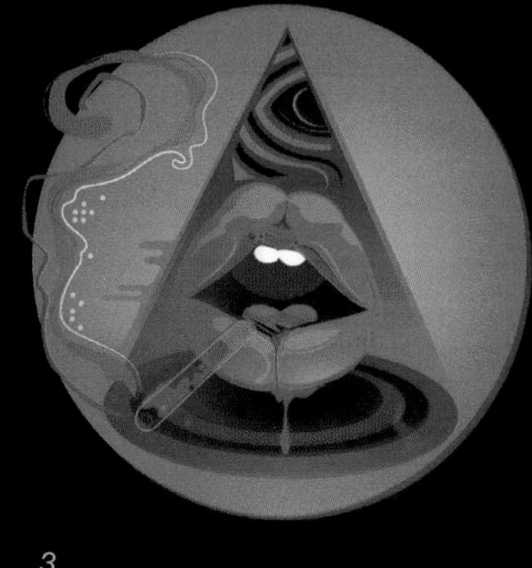

3

1. *Mart Biemans,* **FEEL IT**
2. *Genaro De Sia Coppola,* **UNA COBRA**
3. *Genaro De Sia Coppola,* **YALP**
4. *Jeff Huang,* **BORN 2 RULE**
5. *Genaro De Sia Coppola,* **SUMMER TRIP**

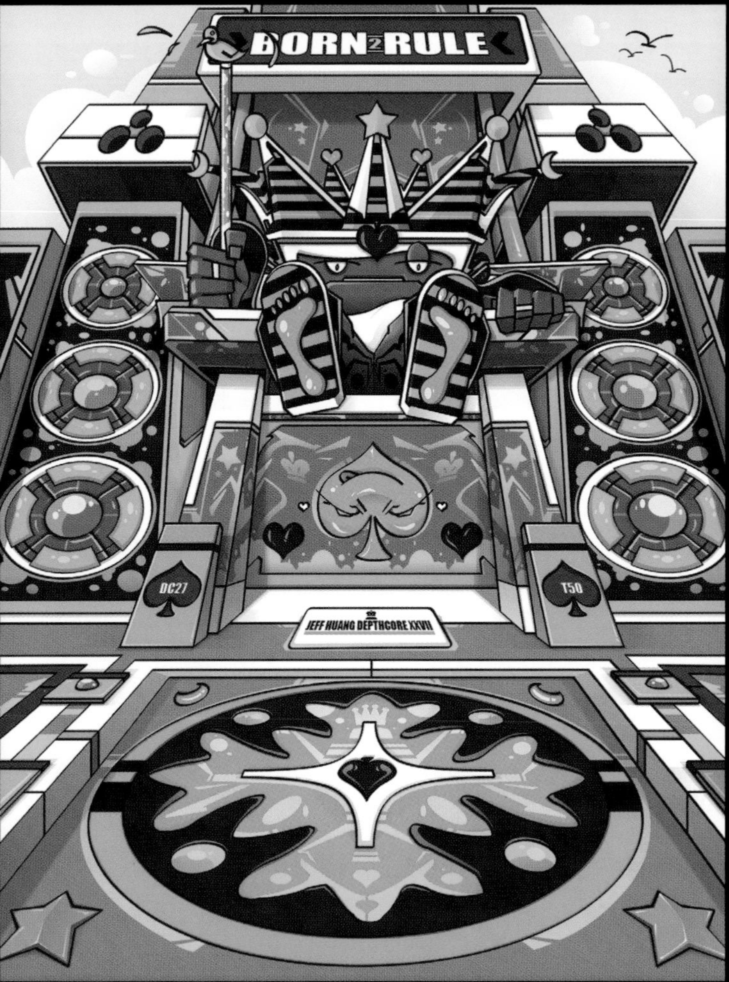

4

5

Interview

Karl Kwasny

Karl Kwasny is a 26-year-old Australian illustrator who studied design at Queensland College of Art. His work has been featured at DeviantART and Oculoid, and can be found on his own website at MONAUX.com. His commercial clients include Coca-Cola, ESPN, MTV, Fox Interactive Media, Hershey's, Nike, Warner Bros. Records, and *Computer Arts, Vibe*, and *Photoshop Creative* magazines. On Abduzeedo.com, Paulo Gabriel wrote of Karl: "He's got a style that I find really dope. Stylish and very detailed, [his work is] a perfect example of the kind of illustration that makes me depressed for not knowing how to do it." Karl is also the author of the tutorial that follows this interview.

How did you start your career as an illustrator? Did you always know that's what you wanted to do?

I think I always knew I wanted to do it; I just didn't know if it was possible. It seemed like such a risky career path, and in many ways it is. You have to be absolutely dedicated to it—dedicated to improving your skills, developing your style, getting work. It's very difficult when you're starting out as an illustrator, trying to get work. I started being serious about it back in 2007. I remember sending five or ten emails a day to companies I wanted to work for. Maybe one in ten would respond, and one of ten responses would result in a job. It's a long road filled with rejection and frustration, but it's such a fulfilling experience once work starts to come in regularly.

How did you come up with your style? What made you explore this style further, and what, in your opinion, are its defining characteristics?

I think it's something that just develops over time. I'm definitely still improving. I'm not quite where I want to be yet, but I hope I'll reach that place in the next few years. I don't think you can "force" a style—it just sort of becomes a collection of things you like, or things you enjoy drawing. I love natural forms, ornate typography, clean lines.

How would you describe your workflow for your projects? How would you break it down into steps?

It depends if I'm working on a project for a client or for myself. Usually, it involves me doodling until I get an idea—thumbnails, roughs, sketches with Photoshop guides if necessary, inks, watercolors, Photoshop touches to finish. If it's work for a client, I just show them the piece at various stages of completion and they provide feedback (and inevitably request amendments).

What role do computers play in your creative process?

I make a point of drawing everything by hand, but computers are certainly helpful for planning out images, coloring, and finishing. I really do use computers a lot even though it may seem as if I don't.

Can you list some artists you admire?

Sure! Albrecht Dürer, Aubrey Beardsley, Barbara Canepa, Alphonse Mucha, Rockin' Jelly Bean, Charles Burns, Gerda Wegener. I could go on...

all of them
MILKING
with
GREEN
fleshy
flowers
&
neutral milk hotel
oh comely
karl

Tell us about some of the works that you are most proud of, and why they are so important for you.

I'm most proud of all the personal drawings I've done for my artbook project so far. I'm always looking forward to the next drawing. I try not to dwell on old ones too much.

Apart from the money you make, what type of satisfaction do you get from your work? And how much does this matter in your life?

I get a huge amount of satisfaction out of completing an image I am proud of. It's like no other feeling in the world.

What advice do you have for those who are just starting their careers? What types of references are important for those who want to work with this kind of style?

It sounds clichéd, but my best advice is "Don't give up." It's easy to get discouraged if companies don't respond to you, or if your work isn't as good as you'd like it to be. All it takes is dedication! If you're determined to improve your art and work hard at it every day, you'll undoubtedly improve. I know I sound like a self-help book, but it's absolutely true. It's also important to be constantly searching for inspiration, looking for interesting applications of illustration, design, and typography. There is so much that goes unnoticed, and so much to find if you look for it.

Tutorial

Illustration by Karl Kwasny

In this tutorial, I will take you through the steps I followed when I created my "Birth Canal" illustration. It's part of an ongoing project I've been developing for some time, so I'll begin with a little background on the project and how "Birth Canal" grew out of it.

Currently, I am working on an artbook project in which I am attempting to create one personal illustration per week for two years. It's proving difficult to find time and inspiration every week amidst work and other commitments, but so far, it has been a very rewarding experience. If you're eager to improve your skills, undertaking deadline-based personal challenges such as this can be very effective. Why not give it a shot?

Step 1

When I begin working on a new idea, I start by doodling for a while until I stumble upon a composition I like and want to take further. In this instance, I already had the idea of using the shape of ovaries as a design element (**1**), so it was just a matter of working out how best to approach the illustration.

Initially, I thought a portrait format would work best, but after sketching for a while it became apparent that landscape was the way to go. This is a fairly symmetrical composition, so I decided that instead of trying to achieve symmetry by eye, I would sketch each element individually and then composite the elements in Photoshop.

Step 2

I sketched a few pose variations until I got one I liked (**2**). For the ovary elements, I decided to print a guide image (an oval and centered vertical line), design one side, scan it, and flip it.

1

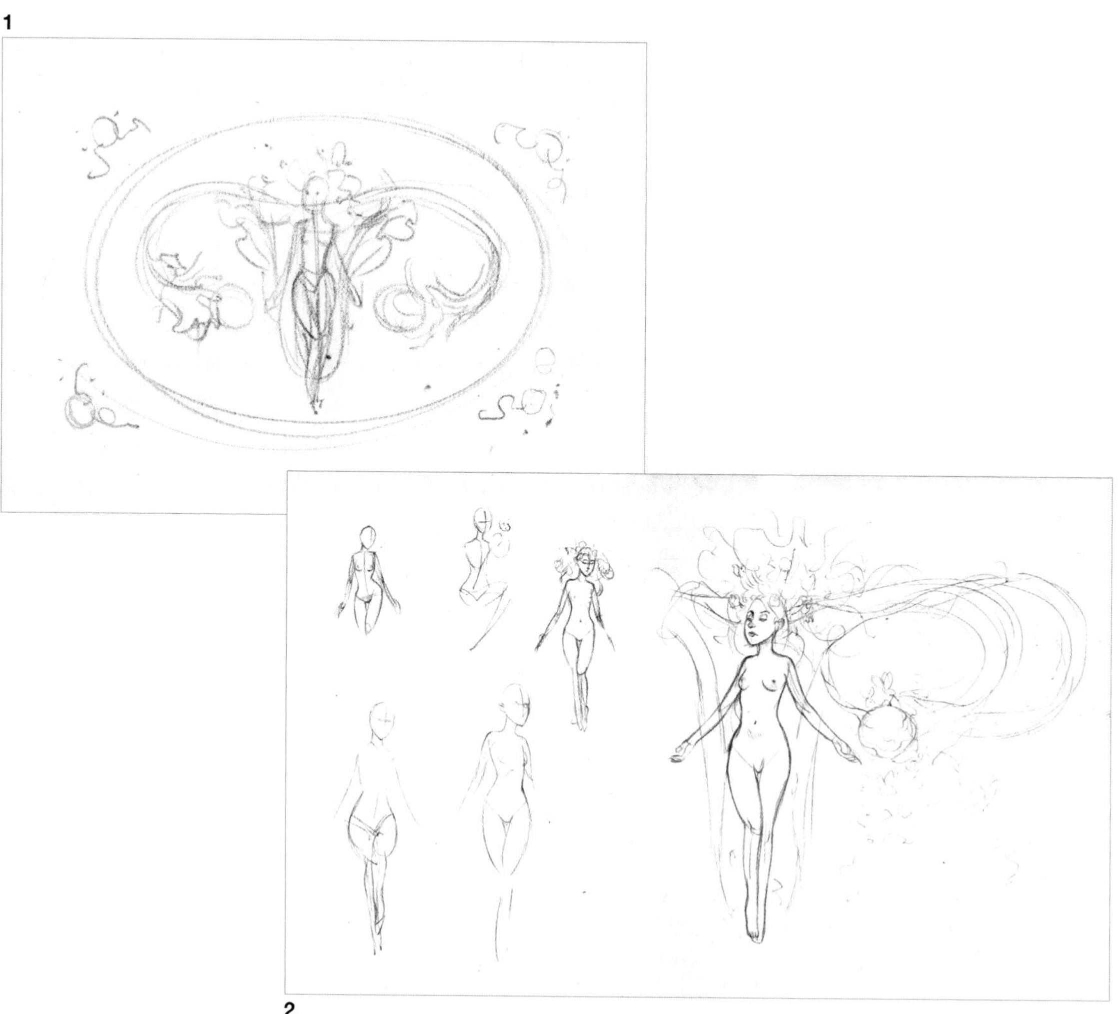

2

Step 3

After I had drawn all the elements, I scanned them all and made the composite guide image (**3**).

At this stage, I should mention that it really helps to use the correct media for the sort of illustration work you're trying to do. For years I drew at A4 size on cheap paper without realizing that I would achieve a much better result if I drew larger and on higher-quality watercolor paper. It's important to experiment and find which medium best suits your work.

Step 4

Once I had the guide image made, I printed it on A3 bond paper and taped it to the back of a sheet of Arches 300gsm hot-pressed watercolor paper. I then refined the rough composite sketch on the watercolor paper with the aid of my lightbox, fixed up anatomy/pose issues, and added detail (**4**).

3

4

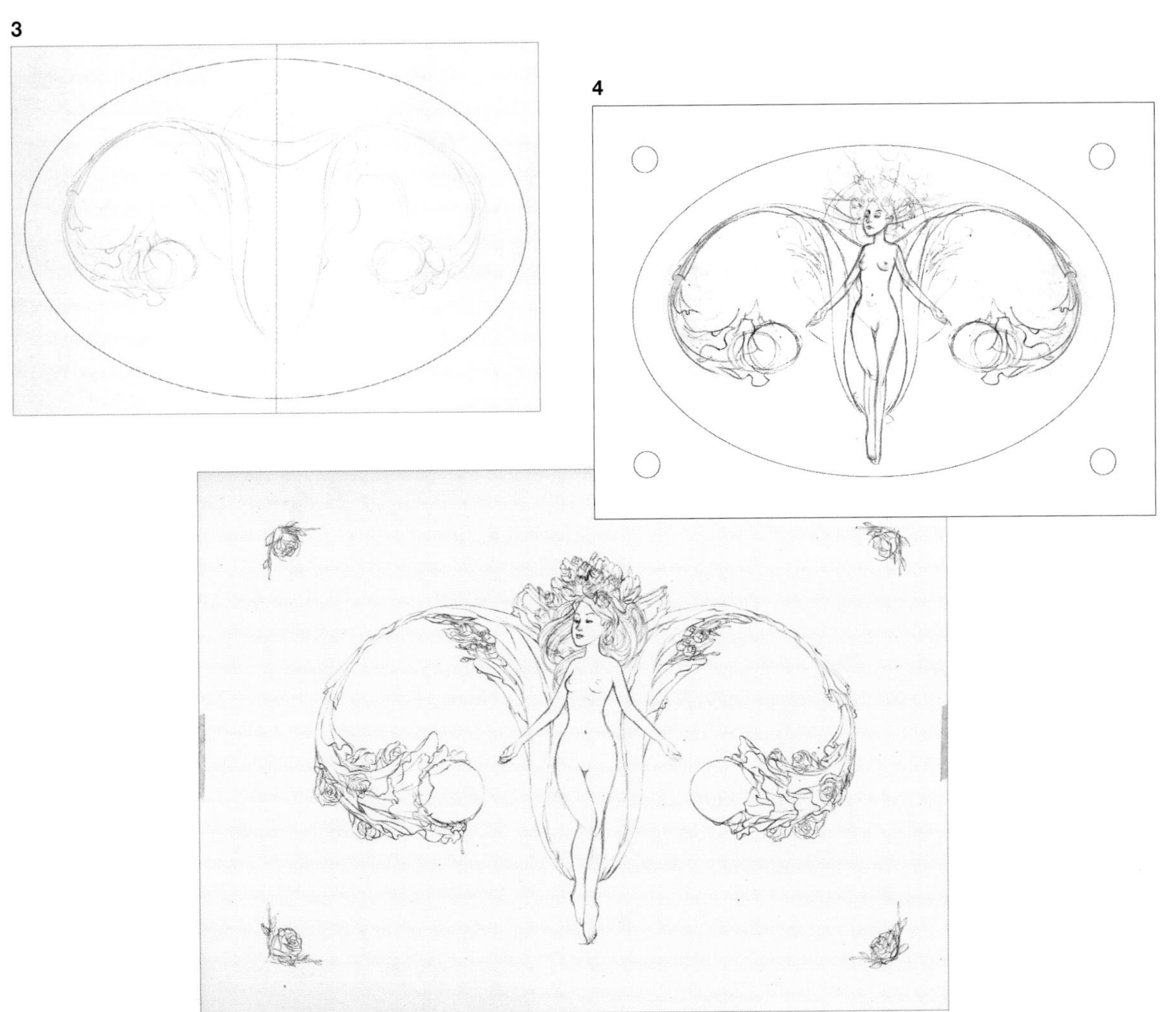

Step 5

I inked the illustration using a #2 Winsor & Newton Series 7 brush and Talon India ink (**5**).

Step 6

My usual process for coloring an image is to use a single color on the original drawing (pink, in this case) and then color sections digitally, using an additional layer over the top of the scanned image set to Color Layer mode in Photoshop (**6**). I recommend experimenting with it! It's possible to get strange, glowing, almost neon effects that are not possible to achieve with actual water colors. Originally, I planned to color this illustration using that method, but once I began working on it I quite liked how it looked as a single color.

Step 7

After I imported the inked and watercolored illustration into Photoshop, I adjusted the levels on the scanned image (**7**). If you move the left and right triangle sliders to a position just before the brightness and darkness spikes start, it brightens the blank paper areas and darkens the blacks without losing any of the definition in the midtones.

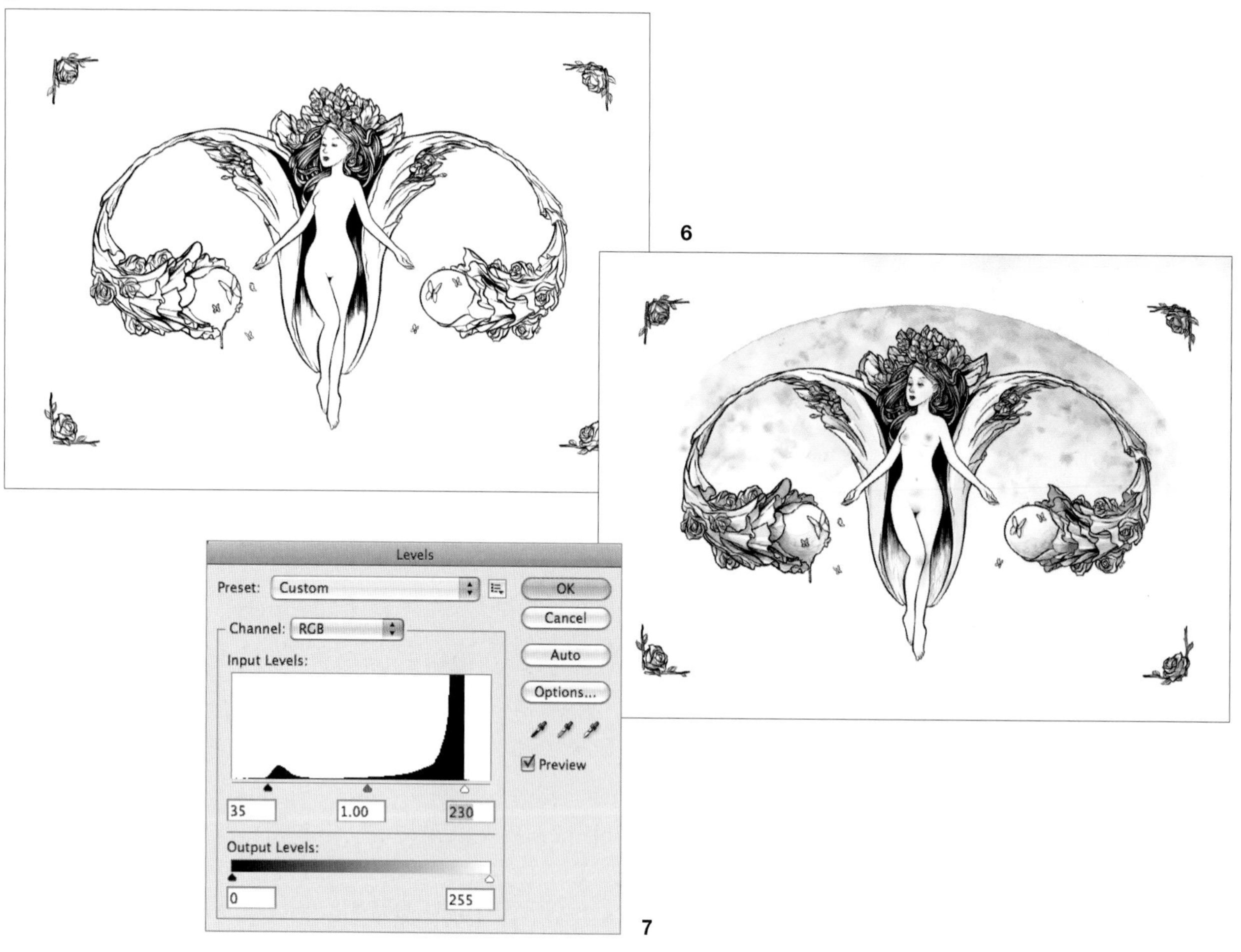

Step 8

At this point, the colors looked a bit too punchy to me and I wanted to subdue them, so I made a dusty pink color layer set to 60% opacity above the scan layer to even them out (**8**).

Step 9

Next, I airbrushed a few of the gram stain-style splotches out because they looked out of place (**9**).

8

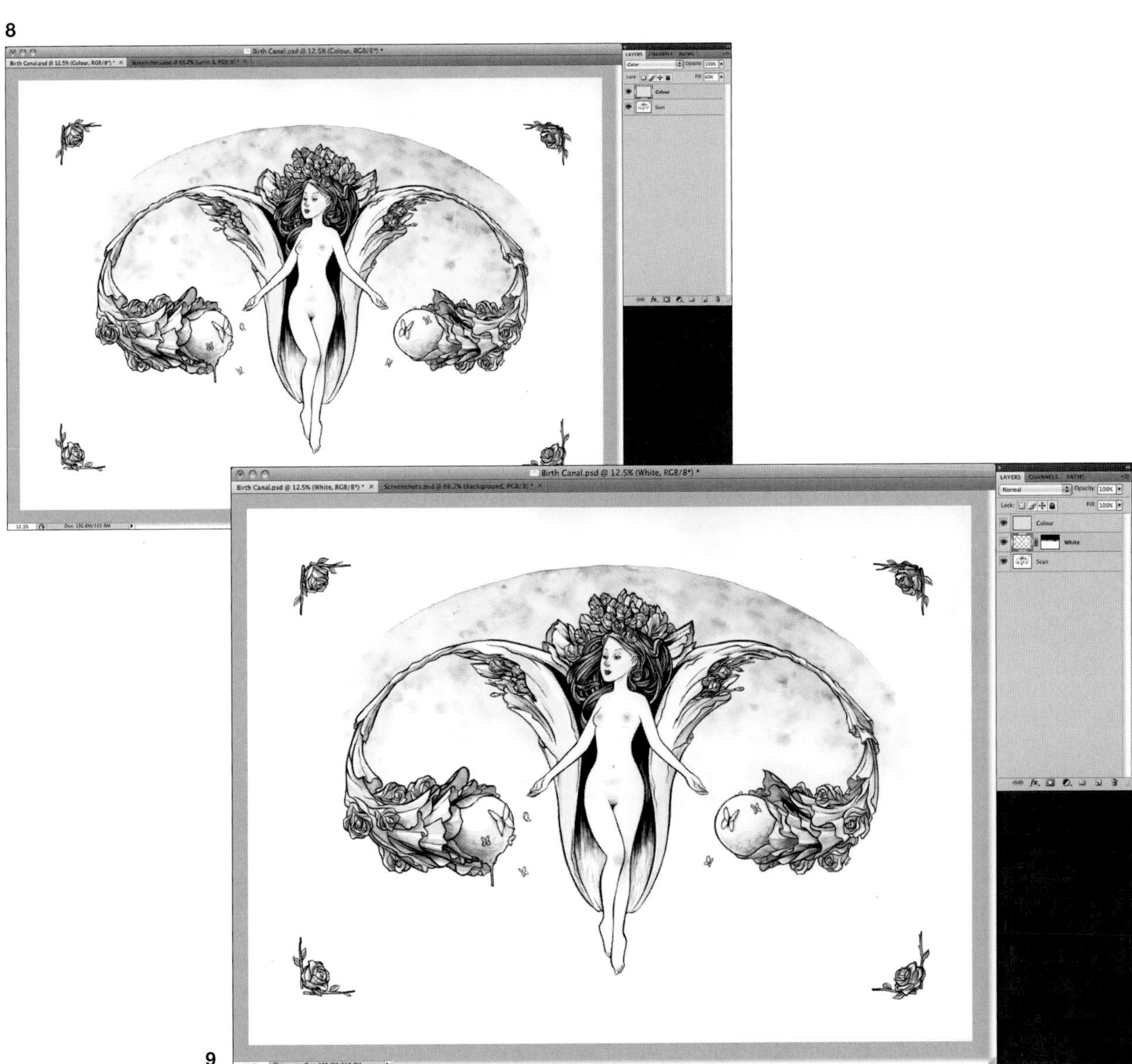

9

Step 10

Although I didn't color the image as I had originally planned, I did end up adding some purple coloring to the shadow areas using a color layer and the airbrush tool with very soft edges (**10**).

Step 11

I decided to fill in the background with a solid color, so I needed to mask out the shape of the woman. I traced around her using the Pen tool and Command-clicked on the layer to select it (**11**).

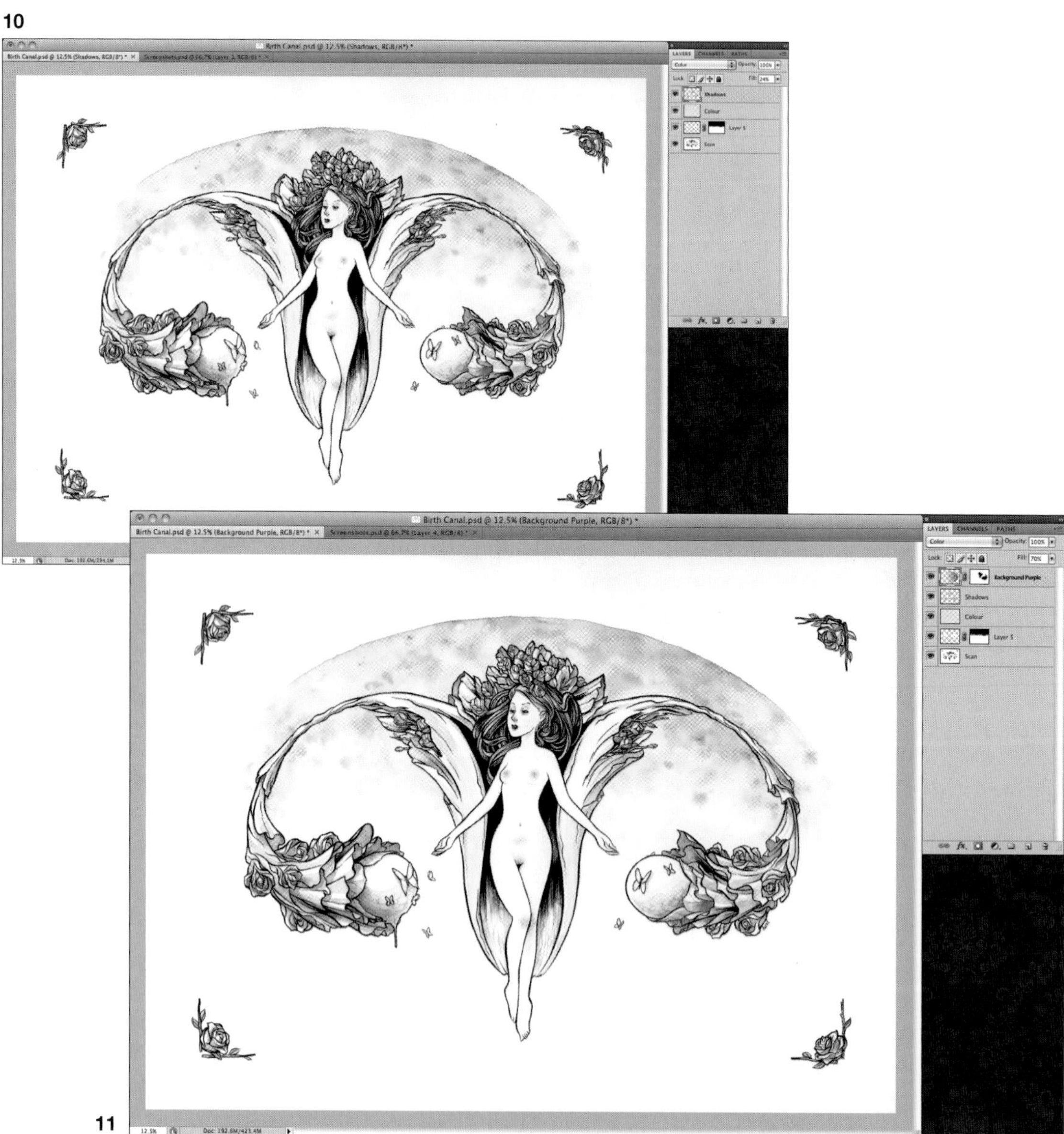

10

11

Step 12

Then I selected the inverse of this mask (Select > Inverse) and made a new layer mask on the pink oval fill layer by clicking the Add Layer Mask button on the bottom of the Layers panel (**12**). Layer masks are definitely one of the most useful parts of Photoshop. It pays to understand how they work! They make it possible to "paint" transparency and opacity onto a layer. I used the Layer mask to create two glowing areas around the ovary orbs by painting two transparent dots with soft edges.

Step 13

After I completed all the color modifications, it was time to clean up. When you scan a piece of paper (particularly if it is dirty or off-white), you'll often find bits that you need to clean up around the edges. I filled a layer with white and subtracted the middle oval shape (**13**).

12

13

Step 14

I copied and pasted the corner rose elements from the scan layer on top of the white fill layer and applied the same color effect as before (**14**).

Step 15

Finally, I decided that I didn't like the look of the perfect Photoshop oval; I wanted an imperfect, hand-drawn one (pedantic, I know). I traced the oval by hand with a fineliner pen onto a new sheet of bond paper using a guide from earlier, scanned it, and applied it as a mask to a white layer on top of everything (**15**).

Conclusion

That's it! I hope you enjoyed this insight into my workflow and took something away that will help you develop a style of working that suits you.

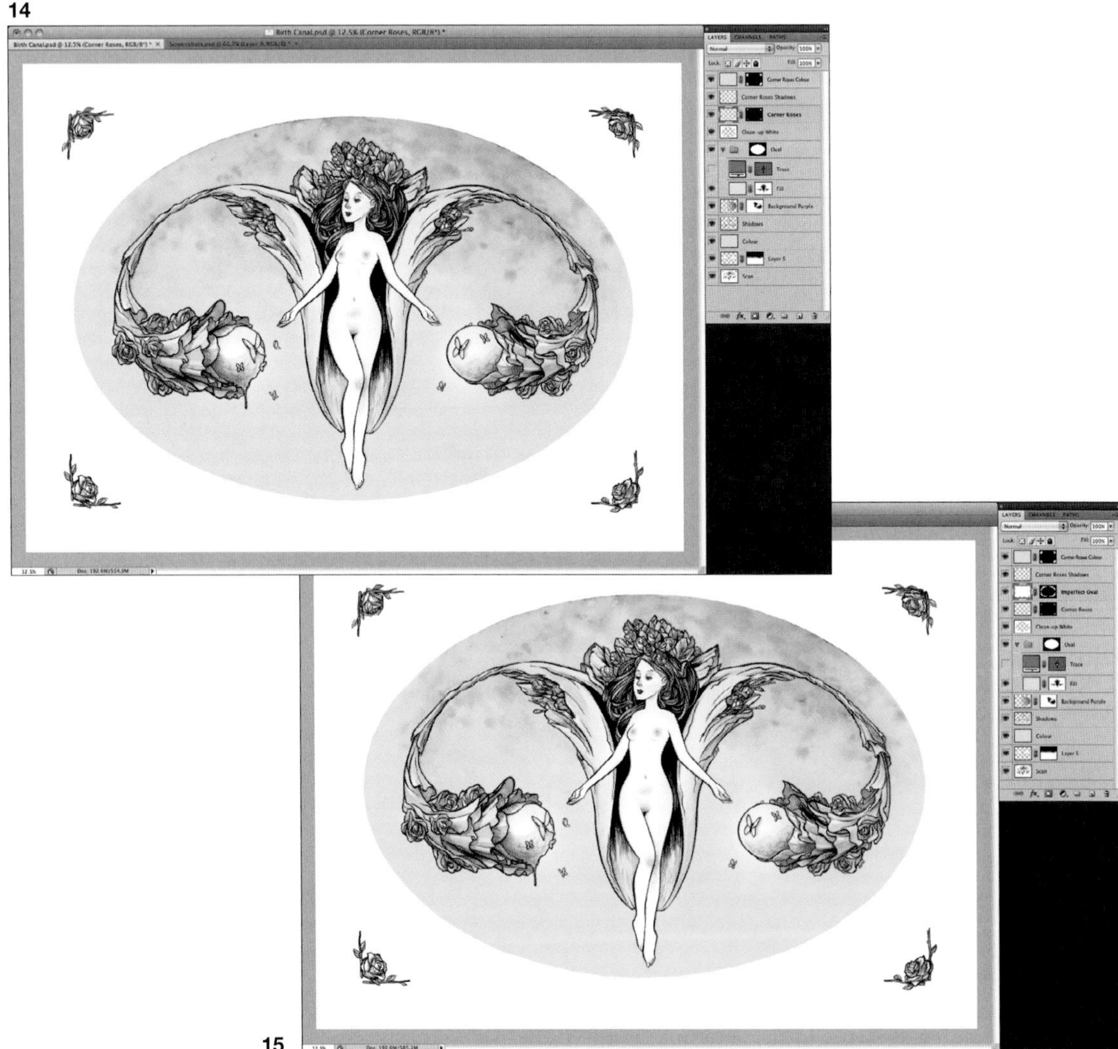

14

15

CHAPTER 4

PHOTO MANIPULATION

Photo manipulation can transform an image much more than subtle changes to the color balance or contrast of a photograph. The resulting image may have little or no resemblance to the picture (or pictures) of origin. Today, photo manipulation is a widely accepted art form. Wikipedia defines photo manipulation as follows:

Photo manipulation is the application of image editing techniques to photographs in order to create an illusion or deception (in contrast to mere enhancement or correction), through analog or digital means.

A,
by Evan Bohringer

Before computers, artists manipulated photos using paint, double exposure, and even by montaging negatives. The 1980s saw the emergence of digital retouching, with computers running software such as Quantel Paintbox, which were later effectively replaced by Adobe Photoshop and other image-editing applications.

In this age of digitization, photo manipulation has become a widespread phenomenon, but it remains a commonly misunderstood and misrepresented topic, associated primarily with the practice of altering images for deceptive purposes. But photo manipulation, in essence, is simply a creative treatment of

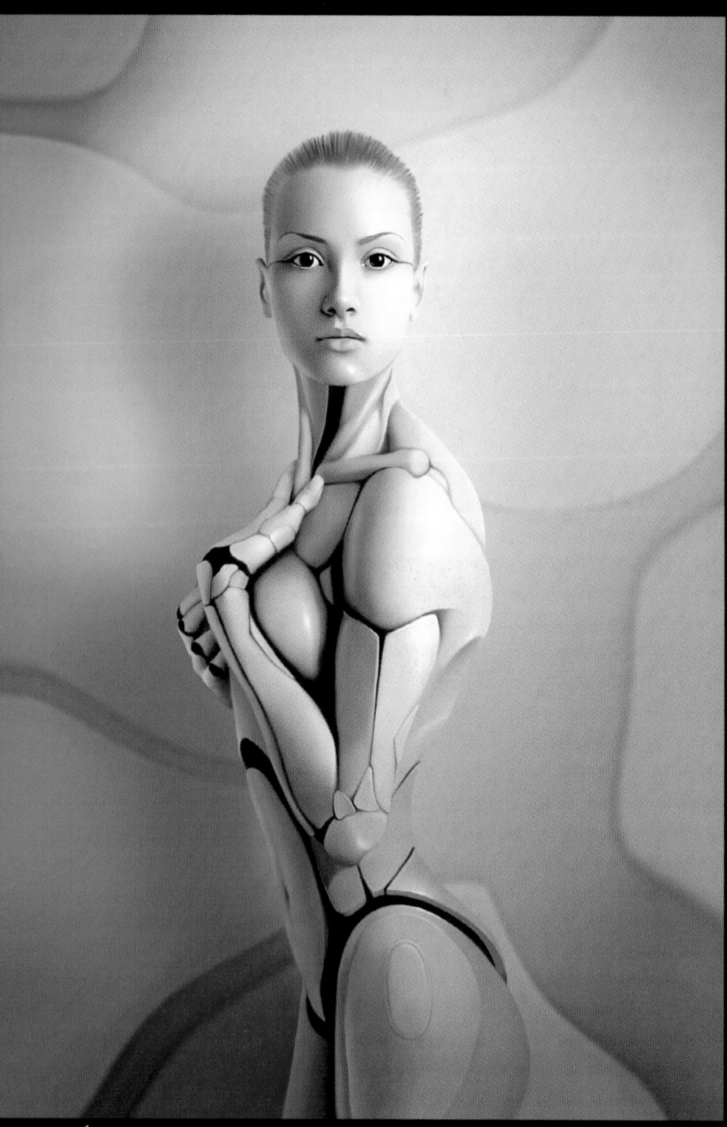

1

2

a digital photograph. Photo manipulation is very often used in fashion and advertising. It's used not only for retouching and altering image elements, but also for changing the image composition, helping to show a message that sometimes isn't possible with a photograph in its original form.

Manipulation, applied artistically, has no intention to deceive, and this becomes even more evident when the work makes clear what is real and what is manipulated. This type of work requires creativity, imagination, and the ability to explore the full potential of digital tools.

4

1. *Michael O,* AMALGAMATE
2. *Michael O,* AMALGAMATE II
3. *Michael O,* DEXTERIA
4. *Michael O,* UNDER MY

1

2

3

4

5

n a post titled "Deceptive Meanings of llusional Photo Manipulation World," Ͻzineblog360 blogger WAQAS E. offers a great take on this topic:

A photographer is an artist, but the art of pho-ography is different from many other arts. It may sound [like an] exaggeration, but you know it when you start learning about it. It is mainly be-cause the idea originates from imagination, but ts execution has to be done in real life. When you take a photo, you have to take an image from real ife and immortalize it. [H]owever, the problem is that … real life isn't exactly known for perfection. From this point the manipulation of an image be-gins and it ends with the final copy of reality de-picting your imagination. The photo manipulation s an art today and it will grow further because with more technological advancement, the room or limning imagination into reality will grow

1. *Fabio Sasso,* ABDUZEEBORG
2. *Fabio Sasso,* UNDERWATER EXPERIMENT
3. *Mart Biemans,* HOME SWEET HOME
4. *Fabio Sasso,* CALL OF ABDUZEEDO
5. *Fabio Sasso,* PHOTOSHOP EXPERIMENT

1

2

3

4

1. *Jeff Huang,* **THE ROTTEN APPLE**
2. *Felix Ajenjo,* **SITTIN' ON TOP**
3. *Jeff Huang,* **THE BECOMING**
4. *Pete Harrison (Aeiko),* **HEARTLESS**
5. *Pete Harrison (Aeiko),* **REQUIEM**

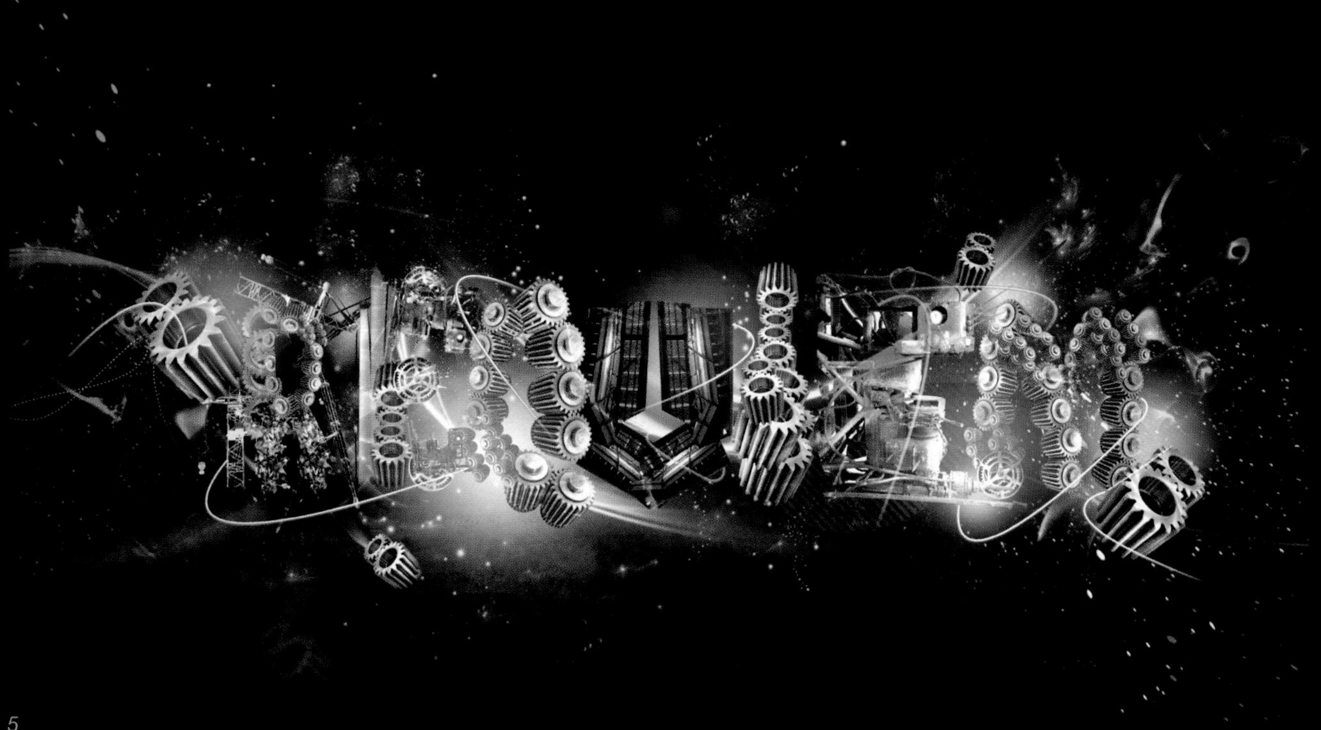

5

1. *Ed Lopez,* **JESTER**
2. *Ed Lopez,* **SPAWN**
3. *Przemek Nawrocki,* **NOT SO COLORFUL**
4. *Rob Shields,* **ENEMY MINE**
5. *Rob Shields,* **THE GOOD REASON FOR OUR FORGETTING**

1

2

3

4

5

Interview

Erik Johansson

Erik Johansson is a professional photographer and photo-retoucher based in Sweden who works on both personal and professional/commercial projects. A former engineering student, he creates photo manipulations that create "a realistic view of an unreal picture," according to Aloa's blog on Abduzeedo.com. Erik shoots with a Canon 5D Mark II and manipulates his photos in Adobe Photoshop CS5. You can see Erik's work online at www.alltelleringet.com.

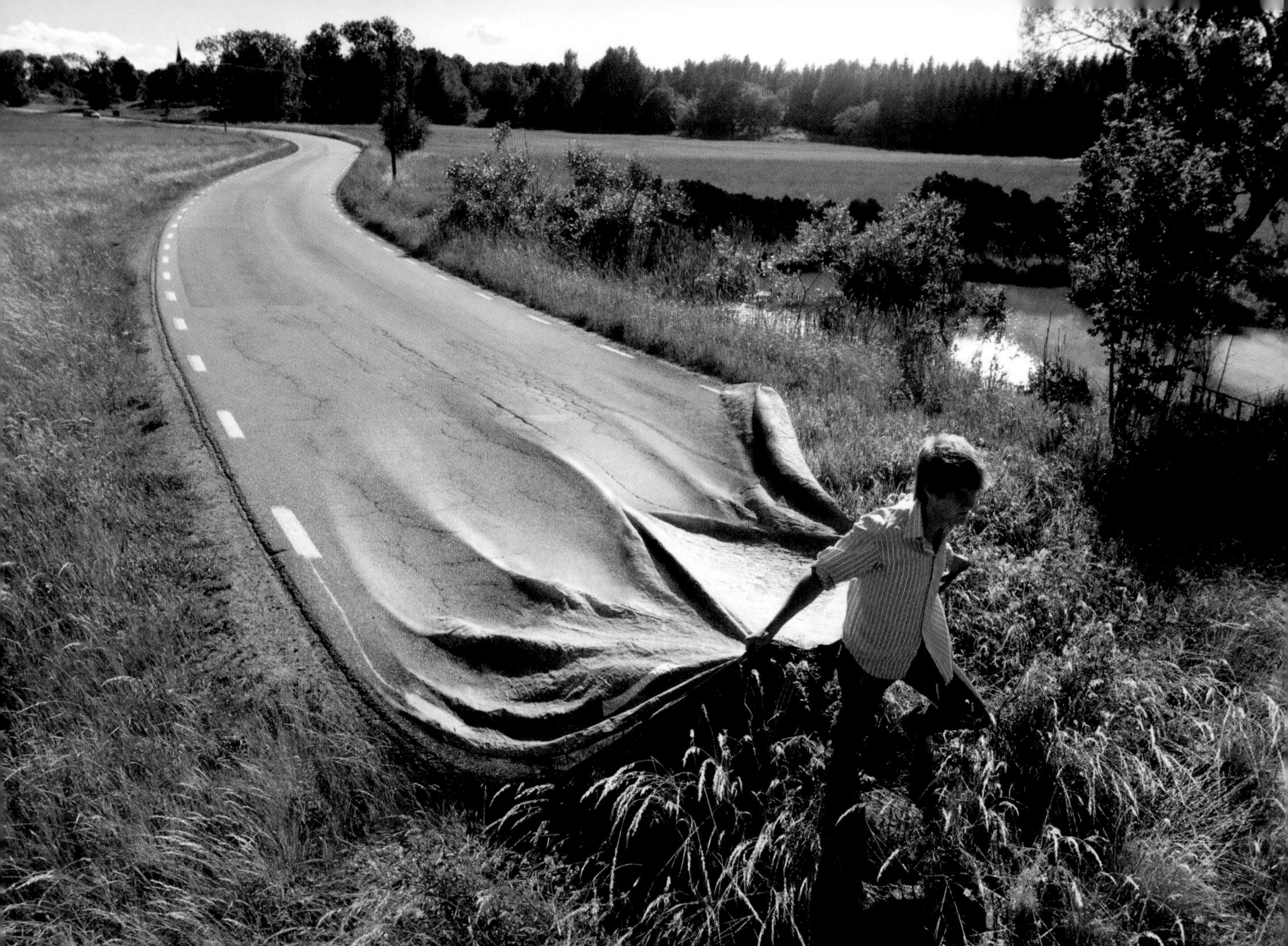

How did you start your career as a digital artist? Did you always know that's what you wanted to do?

I've been drawing for as long as I can remember. As a kid, when my parents asked me how my day in school was, I would rather draw to explain than explain it in words. Early on, I developed an interest in computers. When I got my first digital camera, it was a natural step to try to use the computer to modify photos in different ways. My way of thinking of photography is similar to drawing; the ideas always start with a sketch and it's a challenge to realize them in a photo that's as realistic as possible. As my photos started to spread over the Internet, I got some work requests, and this hobby started to become more and more of a job. Today I'm working on both personal and commercial projects. My personal projects have always been important to me since I can do the projects I feel like working with. The commissioned work is also a challenge in a different way.

How did you come up with your style?

I haven't really decided what I want my style to look like. I just do what feels right and the style becomes a product of my imagination. My ideas are often twisted and surreal, but my goal is always to realize them in a way that's as realistic as possible. I think the characteristic of my style is that I want to make it look like it "could" be true, although some ideas are more unrealistic than others.

How would you describe your project workflow? How would you break down your workflow in steps?

It always starts with an idea that I make a quick sketch of. Usually, I let it rest for a while to come up with small improvements and make it better. Most of the ideas don't make it beyond this point. But if the idea feels right and I think it could be realized in a nice way, I take it to the next step.

The next step is to find places and material that I can photograph to realize the idea. The photos are my material, just like the colors for a painter. The last part is where I put everything together. The time it takes to create this kind of montage depends on the number of photos and the complexity of each part, similar to a puzzle. I usually can't do the montage in one sweep. It's good to let it rest for a while to see it with new eyes a few days later.

What role does the computer play in this creative process?

If I could draw very photorealistically, I wouldn't have to use the computer at all. It's just a tool that helps me to realize my ideas. I don't see it as a part of the creative process. But of course it's an important tool, as my drawing skills aren't as good as my retouching skills.

Could you list some artists/designers you admire?

I actually am more influenced by artists than photographers—Salvador Dali, M.C. Escher, Rob Gonsalves, and René Magritte, to mention a few. I've always been fascinated by illusions and how they mess with your brain. M.C. Escher is one of the best in this area, and many of my impossible pictures are influenced by his work, although I always try to come up with original variations on the theme. Inspiration is something that I get from almost everywhere.

Tell us about some of your works that you are proudest of, and explain why they are so important to you.

I always look forward; I don't really like to look at what I have done, but rather think of what I can do. It's a curse, in a way, but it also helps me to explore new ideas and become better and better.

Apart from the money you make, what type of satisfaction do you get from your work? And how much does this matter in your life?

My personal projects are very important for me. It just feels like something that I have to do. I don't want to force a message upon my viewers; rather, I think that the message should be interpreted by the viewers themselves. Even though my photos don't change the world, I hope that they can inspire people or make them think, just as I get inspired by others.

Commissioned work is not always as creative, as it's limited by the message the client wants to express, but it's also a challenge to realize someone else's idea. I don't think I will ever give up working with personal projects; they're my creative outlet.

What advice do you have for those who are starting out in their careers?

I think that trying is the best way of learning. I recommend experimenting a lot and trying to find your own style. Doing a lot of personal projects doesn't generate much direct income, but it helps to show others what you are capable of.

TETRIS
CONSTRUCTIONS SINCE 1985

Tutorial

Milky Bride in Photoshop

Photo manipulation is all about mixing images in a way that they don't look like they're from different sources. You can create some bizarre effects like Erik Johansson does by playing with photos to achieve unexpected and often funny results.

In this tutorial I will show you how to create a bride with a wedding dress made out of milk. The purpose of this exercise is to show you how to mix images in the most realistic way possible.

Step 1

To begin, open Photoshop and create a new document (**1**). Fill the background layer with black using the Paint Bucket tool (G).

Step 2

Next, add a stock photo. The one I am using comes from Shutterstock, and you can download it here: www.shutterstock.com/pic-70183345/stock-photo-bride-at-night-on-the-beach.html. Using the Lasso tool or the Pen tool and paths, select only the bride and delete the background (**2**). Remember that Photoshop CS5 has a super-improved Refine Edges tool that makes it much easier to extract the background.

Step 3

Once you have removed the background and isolated the bride, choose Layer > Layer Mask > Reveal All. Then, using the Brush tool (B) and a very soft brush with black selected as the color, paint over some parts of the dress to hide them (**3**).

1
2
3

Step 4

Choose Image > Adjustment > Levels. Change the white input to 226 and the gray input to 1.53 (**4**).

Step 5

Duplicate the bride's layer (**5**).

Step 6

Choose Filter > Other > High Pass. Use 3.0 pixels for the Radius setting. Then change the Blend Mode setting of this layer to Soft (**6**).

4

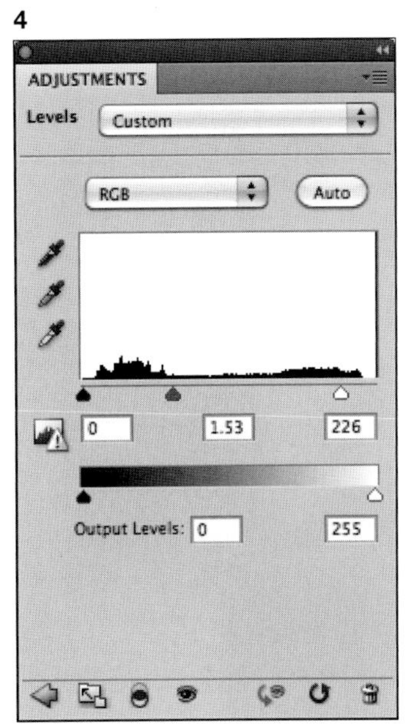

5

6

Step 7

Now let's import some more stock photos, this time using images of milk splashes. The images I am using are all courtesy of Shutterstock, and you can find them at the following URLs:

- www.shutterstock.com/pic-57731110/stock-photo-milk-splash-in-the-air.html
- www.shutterstock.com/pic-57731107/stock-photo-milk-splash-in-the-air.html
- www.shutterstock.com/pic-36258220/stock-photo-splashing-milk.html

Isolate the milk splashes from the background and them place them directly below the bride (**7**). The idea is to create a new dress made out of those splashes.

Step 8

Import another milk splash and position it on the other side. You can select Edit > Transform > Warp to distort the splash to achieve the effect you want (**8**).

Step 9

Use one more milk splash here to finish the dress. Note that you will have to use the Eraser tool (E) to make the transition of the milk and the bride's dress smooth and realistic (**9**).

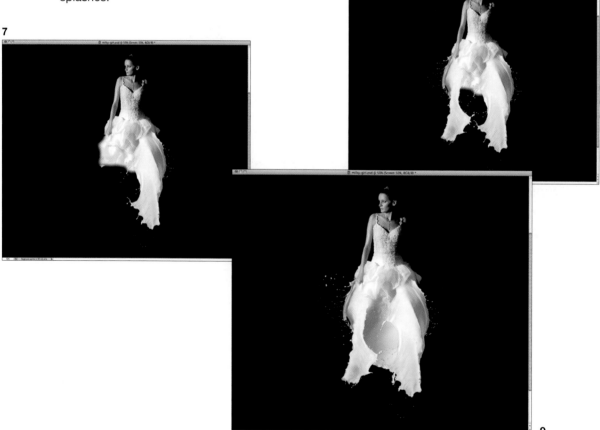

7

8

9

Step 10

Now let's import another image, this time of a hand pouring a glass of milk. You can find the image here: www.shutterstock.com/pic-61137037/stock-photo-hand-pouring-glass-of-the-milk.html.

Place it in front of the other layers (**10**). Notice that the transition of the milk and dress is not right, so now it's time to use the Eraser tool (E).

Step 11

Using the Eraser tool (E), delete parts of the milk of the hand layer so both images are blended together realistically (**11**).

Step 12

Choose Layer > New Adjustment Layer > Hue and Saturation. This adjustment layer has to be on top of the other layers. Change the Hue value to 34 and the Saturation setting to 23 (**12**).

10

11

12

Step 13

Select all layers and duplicate them by using the keyboard shortcut Command/Ctrl+Alt+ Shift+E (**13**).

Step 14

Select the new layer with all the layers merged into it and choose Filter > Blur > Gaussian Blur. Use 15 pixels for the Radius setting (**14**).

Step 15

Change the Blend Mode to Soft Light, and then duplicate the layer. Select the layer that is on top and change its Screen setting to 50%. This screen layer will create a nice glow effect that will help blend together the parts of your composite image (**15**).

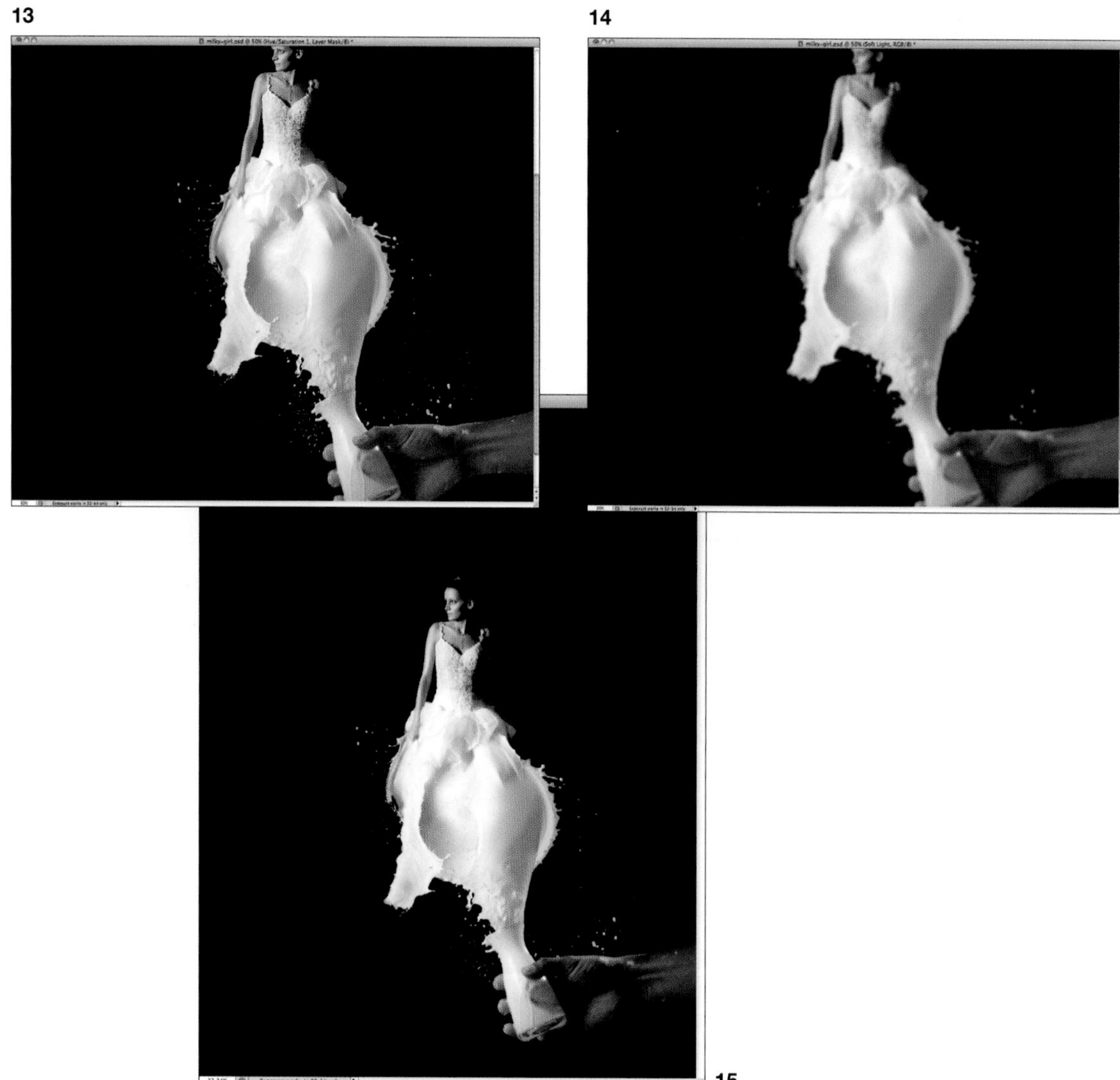

13

14

15

Conclusion

The purpose of this tutorial was to show you how to mix photos to create an unexpected effect, such as a wedding dress made out of milk. As you can see, the most important challenge was to find the right images and to make the adjustments necessary to blend them together in the most realistic way.

Blend modes and adjustment layers are key for this type of effect. Keep working with these tools to become comfortable using them and don't stop practicing.

CHAPTER 5

LIGHT EFFECTS

Light effects became very common in the 1980s as a way of achieving different aesthetic effects in images and, at the same time, as a means of bringing enjoyment and movement to visual spaces. In particular, I'm talking about bold light effects, rather than subtle adjustments—super-bright spaces with a lot of colors and shapes of light, the sort of light effects that marked the psychedelic era.

Wikipedia defines light effects, also known as lighting and illumination, as follows:

Lighting or illumination is the deliberate application of light to achieve some aesthetic or practical effect. Lighting includes use of both artificial light sources such as lamps and natural illumination of interiors from daylight.

CITY LIGHTS,
by Pete Harrison (Aeiko)

With the evolution of computer graphics in the late 1980s, artists began to explore the possibilities for applying light effects in digital imagery, albeit tentatively at first, perhaps because of the constraints that limited system resources imposed. By the end of the '80s, graphic design was undergoing an unmistakable shift from the use of mechanical techniques for producing photos to a digital, computer-based approach, making it easier than ever to create graphic images with text, illustrations, photos, and colors. However slowly light effects may have progressed in the early years of computer-aided design, the fact is that the designers of the 1980s started this new wave in design and architecture, and the evolution of the form since then has been incredible.

1

2

Pete Harrison (Aeiko), **FRUCTIV**

Pete Harrison (Aeiko), **OUTBREAK**

Pete Harrison (Aeiko), **LURE**

Pete Harrison (Aeiko), **OAHU**

Pete Harrison (Aeiko), **SOUL**

1

2

1. *Fabio Sasso,* LIGHT EFFECTS EXPERIMENT
2. *Pete Harrison (Aeiko),* SUGAR
3. *Fabio Sasso,* FLYING GIRL
4. *Pete Harrison (Aeiko),* SUPERHIGHWAY

abduzeedo

3

abduzeedo

1

2

3

1. *Fabio Sasso,* **POSTER—2K10**
2. *James White,* **ATARI**
3. *James White,* **SMASHING**
5. *James White,* **TRON (2)**
6. *James White,* **TRON (3)**
7. *Fabio Sasso,* **LENS FLARE**

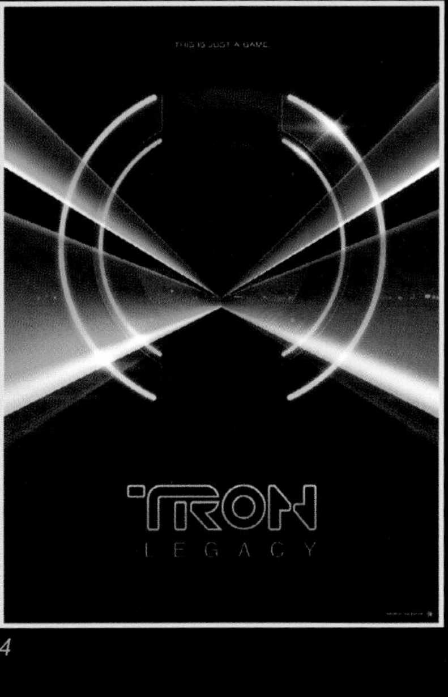

4

5

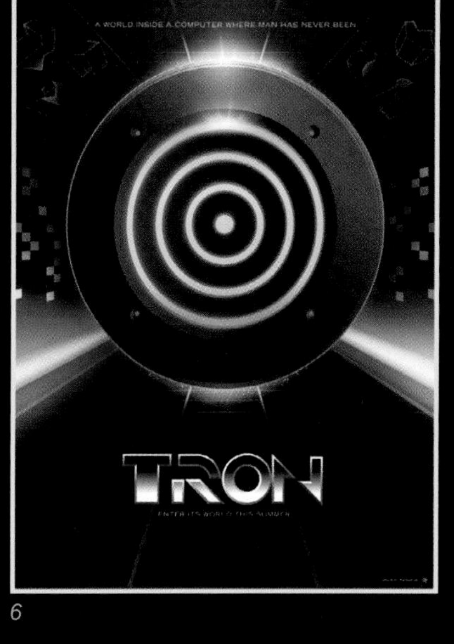

6

In today's graphic design, light effects are often used to create a more accurate depiction of reality, but their main purpose is to transcend the limits of reality, bringing movement and life to an element that could initially be isolated within a scene. These reality-altering light effects can communicate or represent creativity, technology, magic, and even fantasy.

The new software-based design applications introduced in the 1990s brought even more ease to the light-effect creation process, and gave designers more resources for taking advantage of the creative possibilities inherent to light effects. Glow and light effects are becoming increasingly popular in design these days. Adding these effects has turned into a habit for many designers and, for that reason, the way they're used is sometimes even a little banal.

That said, we have great examples of designers around the world using light effects imaginatively and purposefully to mark their work, including artists such as Chuck Anderson, as well as James White and me, who are featured in this chapter's gallery.

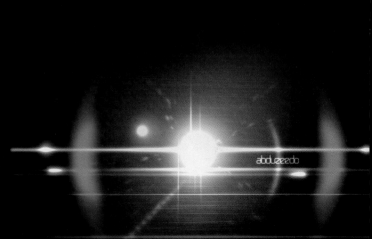

1

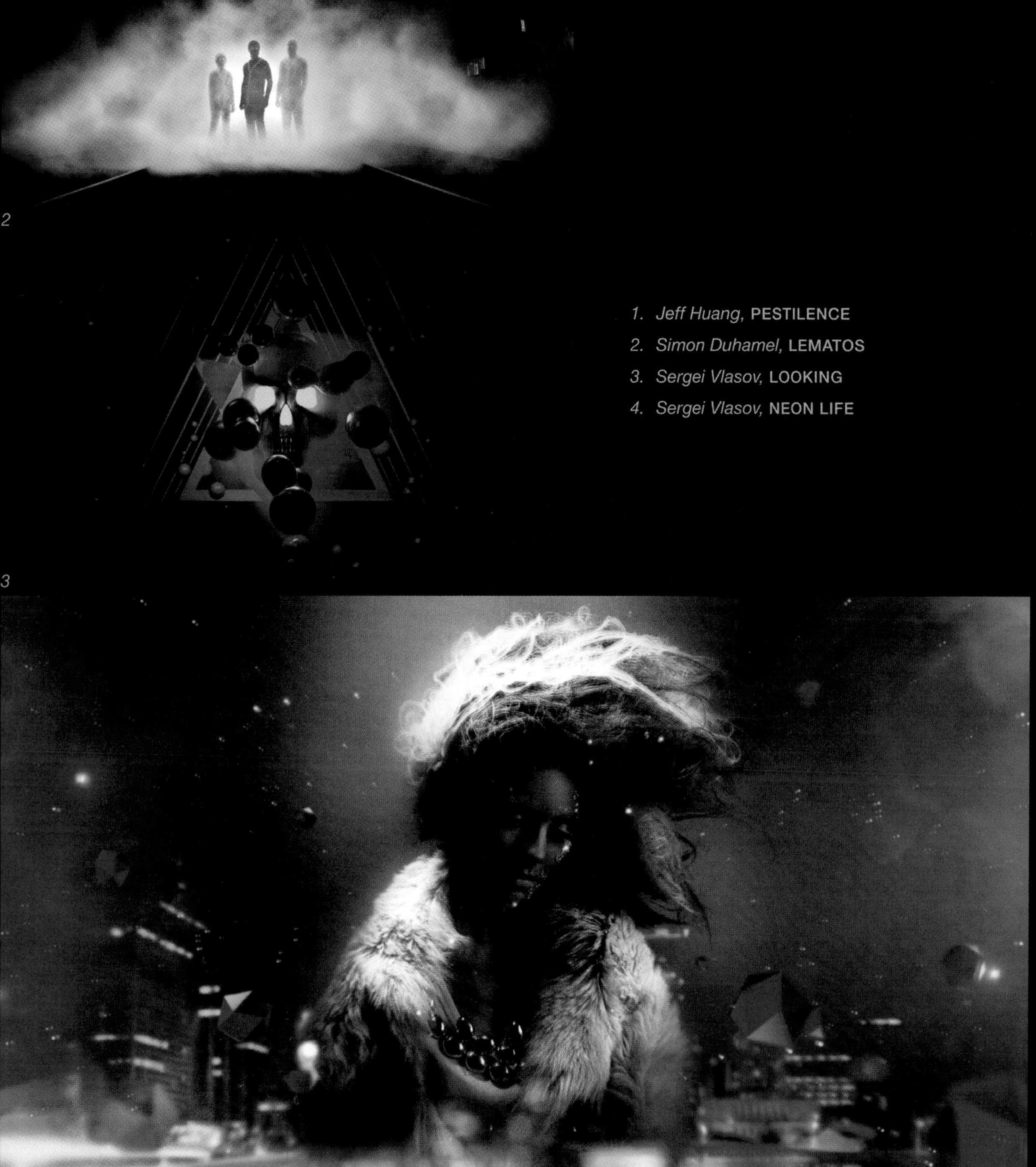

2

3

1. *Jeff Huang,* **PESTILENCE**
2. *Simon Duhamel,* **LEMATOS**
3. *Sergei Vlasov,* **LOOKING**
4. *Sergei Vlasov,* **NEON LIFE**

Interview

Chuck Anderson

Chuck Anderson is a Chicago-born graphic designer and illustrator based in Grand Rapids, Mich. His NoPattern studio (www.nopattern.com) has served a range of clients, including Warner Bros., Nike, Pepsi, 555Soul, Microsoft, Sony, Garcia Marquez, ESPN, Vans, and Reebok.

How did you start your career as a digital artist and designer? Did you always know that you wanted to work in this field?

I've been an artist to some degree my entire life, starting all the way back when I was just a little kid. I loved to draw; I loved to get drawing books from the library; I loved to doodle in class. Everything about the process of creating something was always something I loved. Eventually and naturally, I was introduced to using a computer for design and then, of course, Photoshop. The progression was organic. I always knew I would make my living as some kind of an artist. The fact that I use a computer and work digitally is not important to me. At the end of the day, the computer is just one of many tools I use.

How did you come up with your style, and what made you explore this style further?

I discovered it out of boredom and a desire to experiment. I've always been fascinated by light, the way light hits certain surfaces, the way it plays with color, and just the beauty in it. I carried that love into my work and have found it really fun to manipulate light, especially in photography.

When I was still living with my parents, I'd go out late at night in my car with my camera and take pictures of empty parking lots, streets, gas stations—anything that looked interesting to me. I lived in the suburbs then, so there wasn't much to photograph unless you really looked hard, and I found beauty in the lights at night. Then it was just

a matter of exploring and experimenting with Photoshop, knowing that nobody could tell me what to do, and that there really were no rules for the type of work I was trying to create.

Can you list some artist and designers who inspired you to get better and better?

Mark Romanek, KAWS, Deanne Cheuk, Nago Richardis, Thomas Hooper, Jacob Bannon, Kimou Meyer, David Shrigley, Mike Giant, James Blagden, Jens Karlsson, Mike Cina, Nathan Flood… All these artists and designers are so different from one another, but there are qualities in all of them personally and in their work that I really admire, love, and look up to. There are many more; those are just some of the names I thought of off the top of my head. The funny thing is that none of them do work that looks anything like mine at all.

How would you describe your workflow for your projects? How would you break it down in steps?

I really don't have a set workflow. It's hard for me to describe because there's not a lot to say. If it's client work, I simply take their brief and direction, and then usually we'll have a creative kickoff call about the job, and after the call I'll just start working on it. Beyond that, on my projects, I don't worry about anything in terms of workflow or a schedule, or working in any sort of structured manner. I just do what I do when I need to do it.

Which part of the process do you like the most: before, when you have only the idea and a vision of what it's going to be like; during, when you actually transform your idea into your creation; or after, when the work is done and you look at the final piece?

I would say there are enjoyable parts of all the stages of creation, but the "during" part is usually the most enjoyable part for me, because that's when I'm doing what I do best. "After" is fun too because I'm done working, and I get to take a break, relax, and see my end result. The "before" part is fun too, conceptualizing and working on the vision for the project. But nothing compares to the actual creative process itself.

How important is the computer in your creative process?

Well, considering that the computer is where I do about 80 percent of my work, I'd say that it's extremely important. It's essential for creation, for business, and communication, for finding inspiration, and for archiving your work. For anyone working today in the creative world, it's almost guaranteed that at some point a computer will come into play in your process.

Apart from the money you make, what type of satisfaction do you get from your work? How much does this matter in your life?

There is huge satisfaction in seeing your commercial work finally printed and out in public. Any time I've done something large, such as a mural or billboard, it's a great feeling to know that thousands and thousands of people are seeing it every single day. The financial benefits of working very hard are great, but there is an unmatchable satisfaction in knowing that you've completed your work successfully and have another good project to add to your body of work.

What advice do you have for those who are just starting out in their careers?

Don't strive to work with only one kind of style. Try to be good at a lot of things, or focus on one thing but continue to explore other types of work and creation. If you really are very interested in light and color, then you need to get to know photography, and get to know color in a fundamental way. Know how colors affect each other, how light and shadows affect each other, and how they affect color. Be sure to place an importance—especially if you are working with photography and are adding effects like I often do—on integrating light and color *into* a photograph, rather than slapping light and color effects on top of a photo as if they have no business being there. Always explore and try new things. It's the only way to grow.

light

Tutorial

Creating a Light Effect in Photoshop

Light effects are my favorite type of effect. I don't know why, but I always liked to play around in Photoshop trying to re-create the effects I saw in others' work. But after I discovered the power of the blend modes—especially the Color Dodge—I found that creating my own light effects became much easier.

In this tutorial I'll show you how to create a super-cool text light effect, while mixing some photos to provide more realism. One great thing about this effect is that the whole process is very simple.

Step 1

To begin, open Photoshop and create a new document. Then make sure that the background color is set to black (**1**).

Step 2

To make the effect more realistic, let's use a stock photo. The one I am using comes from Shutterstock, and you can find it at www.shutterstock.com/pic-24939406/stock-photo-glowing-lamp-on-black-background.html. Place the image in the center of the document, but make sure that the filament area is big enough (**2**).

Step 3

Choose Layer > Layer Mask > Reveal All. Then, with the Brush tool (B), select a very soft brush (0% hardness), and choose black for the color. Start painting the areas of the light you want to hide (**3**).

Step 4

Now let's delete the filament area where we will add the text with the light effect later on. It's a pretty easy process. With the Eyedropper tool (I), select the color of the area you will paint. Then, using the Brush tool (B) and a very soft brush, start

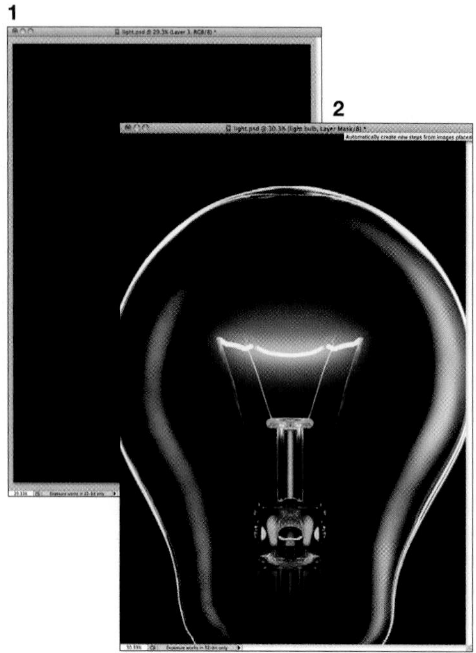

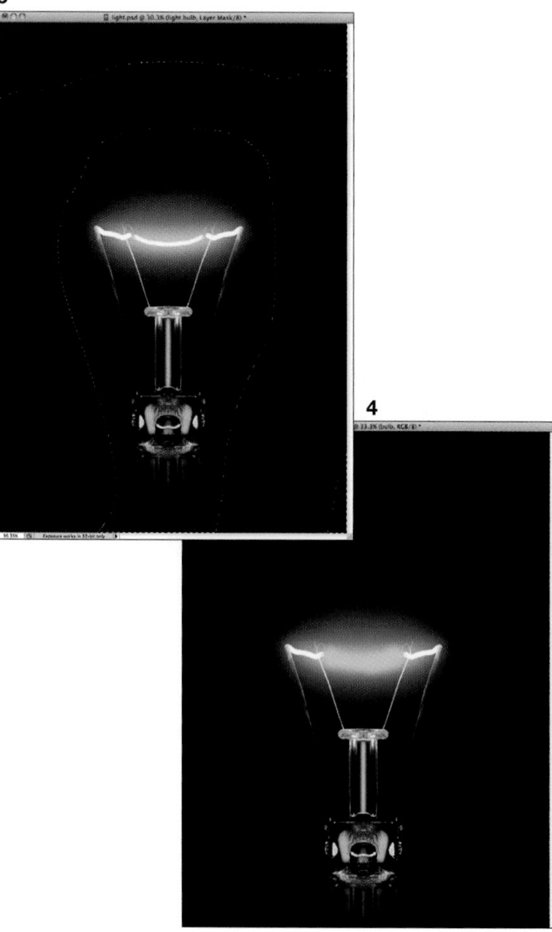

painting over the filament. Note that I added a new layer instead of painting over the light in the same layer (**4**). Another tip is if you're working with the Brush tool, you can press Alt at any time to use the Eyedropper.

Step 5

Select the Horizontal Type tool (T), choose white as your text color, and type *light* (**5**). In this example. I'm using a font called Exmouth, which you can download at www.dafont.com/exmouth.font. For the size of my text, I've chosen 82 pixels, but the size of the text in your image will depend on your document size.

After typing in the text, add a new folder in the Layers palette and change the blend mode of this folder to Color Dodge. Move the light text into the folder you have just created.

Step 6

With the text selected, choose Filter > Blur > Gaussian Blur. Use 4 pixels for the Radius setting (**6**).

Step 7

Because the white text is inside the folder with the Color Dodge, the effect will be the same as if the text layer had a black background. Note that the edges blend with the background, creating a perfect light effect (**7**).

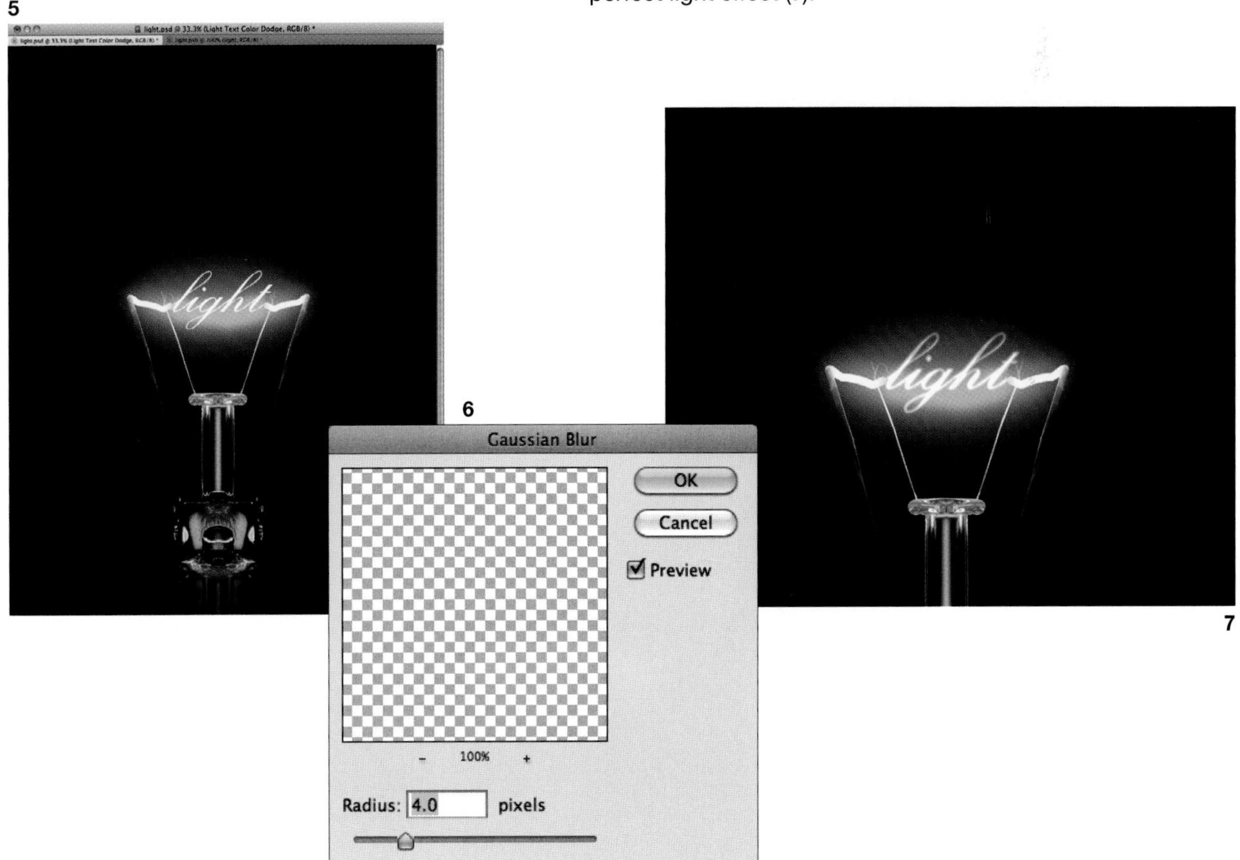

Step 8

Again, to add more realism, instead of creating a lens flare in Photoshop, we'll use a real photo. I found the one I'm using via Google Images. You can download it here: http://web.williams.edu/astronomy/IAU_eclipses/jmp_eclipse03_04.jpg.

Once you have imported the photo, delete the areas that you won't need, keeping just the flare. Then choose Image > Adjustments > Desaturate (**8**).

8

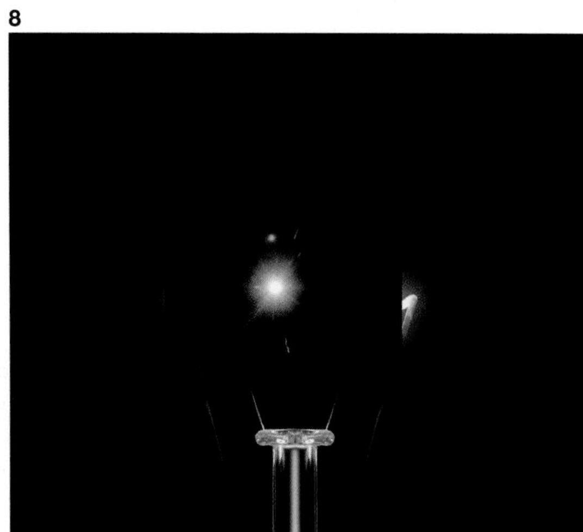

Step 9

With the flare layer already desaturated, change its Blend Mode setting to Screen. Screen turns a black background back into full transparency by making the grayscale a transparency level (**9**). It's perfect for creating light effects.

Step 10

Next, add a new layer and choose Filter > Render > Clouds. Make sure you have black and white selected as the background and foreground colors, respectively (**10**). This layer also will be placed on top of the others.

10

9

Step 11

Change the Blend Mode setting for the clouds layer to Color Dodge. Then add a new folder in the Layers palette and move the clouds layer into it (**11**). Change the new folder's Blend Mode setting to Overlay.

Step 12

Add a new layer inside the folder where you just moved the clouds layer. Make sure that the new layer is positioned beneath the clouds layer. Then, using the Brush tool (B) and a very soft brush with #f5d38b selected as your color, paint a round spot in the center of the light effect (**12**). Change this layer's Blend Mode setting to Overlay too.

Step 13

Now add another layer on top of all the others. Using the Brush tool (B) and a big and very soft brush, select white for the color, and paint another big spot in the center of the light effect. Next, choose Layer > Layer Style > Color Overlay. Use color #ffd648 and apply a Linear Burn. The idea is to make the light a bit stronger. Now our effect is complete (**13**).

Conclusion

As you can see, most light effects are all about blending colors with photos. The blend modes in Photoshop are very powerful for this type of effect, and you should study these modes carefully, especially Color Dodge, as you continue your exploration of light effects.

11

12

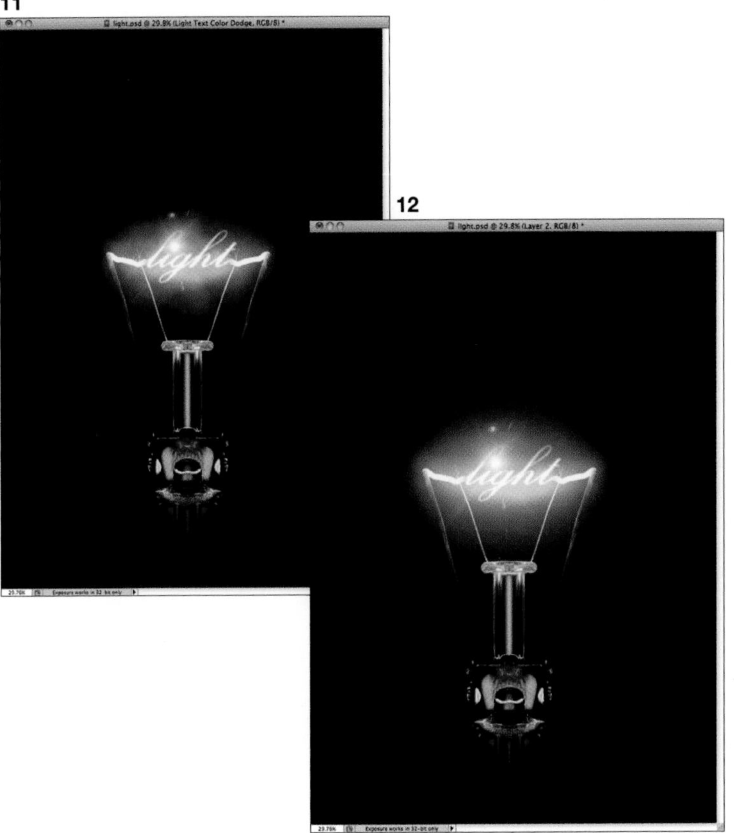

13

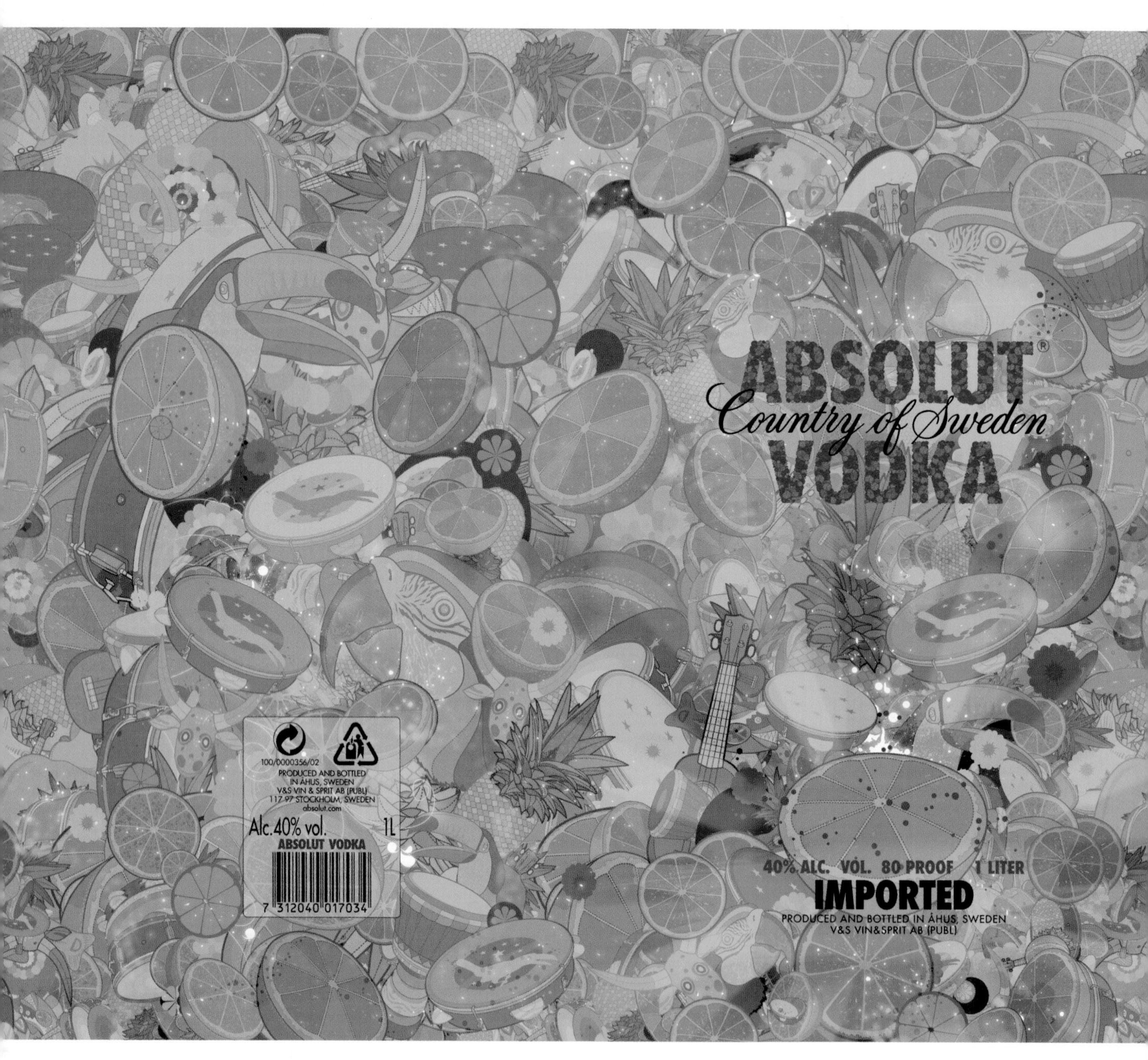
ABSOLUT®
Country of Sweden
VODKA
40% ALC. VOL. 80 PROOF 1 LITER
IMPORTED
PRODUCED AND BOTTLED IN ÅHUS, SWEDEN
V&S VIN&SPRIT AB (PUBL)
100/0000356/02
PRODUCED AND BOTTLED
IN ÅHUS, SWEDEN
V&S VIN & SPRIT AB (PUBL)
117 97 STOCKHOLM, SWEDEN
absolut.com
Alc.40% vol. 1L
ABSOLUT VODKA
7 312040 017034

CHAPTER 6

VECTOR ART

Graphic design has been used to convey messages through images, symbols, and more recently, words. Vectors were always there to make up the elements of these messages, eons before we worked with them in digital form. On Wikipedia, contemporary vector graphics is defined as follows:

Vector graphics is the use of geometrical primitives such as points, lines, curves, and shapes or polygon(s), which are all based on mathematical equations, to represent images in computer graphics.

Vector art is the secret to good design. In digital design, it's essential to be able to create work that can be printed in several larger sizes without blurring, like creating a logo for a booklet and then using this same element for a billboard. Vectors make this possible. The use of vectors has completely changed the way graphic designers conceive and create their projects.

ABSOLUT,
by Guilherme Marconi

Over time, vector-based design applications have become increasingly powerful. Today's artists can create vectors with numerous editing tools, incorporating knots, points, and lines. We can even manipulate these elements to create surreal images, applying photographic effects and even 3D.

The ability to rasterize images, also known as rotoscoping, allows us to use a photo as the foundation of a digital image and turn everything in it into vectorized elements. But today's designers are not content simply to transform something into vectors; we want to add new elements to scenes, such as merged vectors and photos, and even lights and vectors that, when properly applied, form an almost perfect composition.

1

2

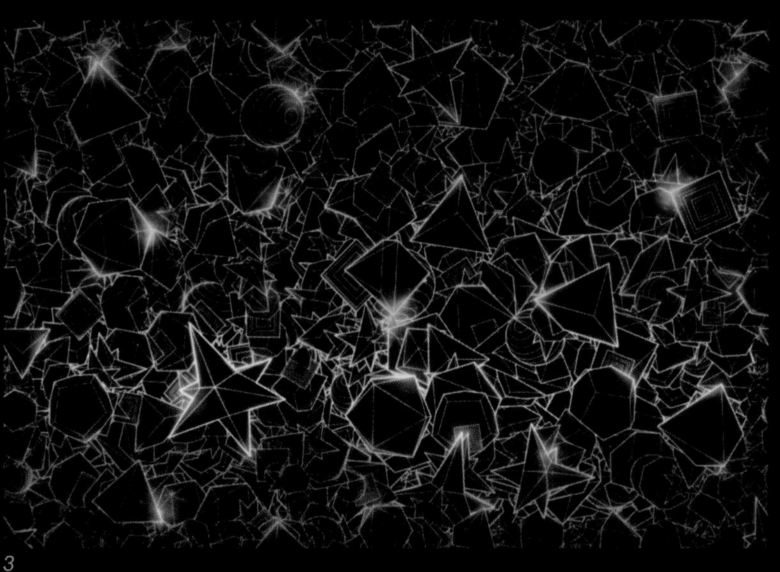

3

1. *Guilherme Marconi,* BASE
2.. *Guilherme Marconi,* CANDY
3. *Guilherme Marconi,* BULLET

The same decisions we make about graphic design also apply in the world of typography. To achieve good print quality, we base today's fonts and typefaces on drawn elements and store them as vector graphics, which allows them to be scaled to any size.

One of the masters of contemporary vector art is Brazilian designer Cristiano Siqueira. The quality of his work is extraordinary. You'll learn about his work process in this chapter's interview and tutorial.

1. *Guilherme Marconi,* CENTRO CULTURO BANCO DO BRASIL (1)
2. *Guilherme Marconi,* CENTRO CULTURO BANCO DO BRASIL (2)
3. *Guilherme Marconi,* CENTRO CULTURO BANCO DO BRASIL (3)

Centro Cultural 20

Brasil um país de todos Governo Federal

20 anos do Centro Cultural Banco do Brasil. Faz diferença ser cliente de um banco que leva cultura para todo o país.

Pensar na cultura do brasileiro é pensar numa riqueza sem igual, onde milhares de formas, cores e ritmos se misturam em uma nação única. Nos Centros Culturais Banco do Brasil você encontra sempre uma programação assim: diversificada, criativa, onde cada brasileiro pode se sentir representado e, principalmente, estimulado.

Banco do Brasil. Faz diferença ter um banco todo seu.

bb.com.br/cultura

BANCO DA CULTURA

2

Centro Cultural 20 anos

Brasil um país de todos Governo Federal

20 anos do Centro Cultural Banco do Brasil. Faz diferença ser cliente de um banco que leva cultura para todo o país.

Pensar na cultura do brasileiro é pensar numa riqueza sem igual, onde milhares de formas, cores e ritmos se misturam em uma nação única. Nos Centros Culturais Banco do Brasil você encontra sempre uma programação assim: diversificada, criativa, onde cada brasileiro pode se sentir representado e, principalmente, estimulado.

Banco do Brasil. Faz diferença ter um banco todo seu.

bb.com.br/cultura

BANCO DA CULTURA

3

1

1. *Guilherme Marconi,* **JAPAN**
2. *Guilherme Marconi,* **KOKESHI**
3. *Guilherme Marconi,* **LINES**
4. *Ari Weinkle,* **JEWEL THIEF**
5. *Ari Weinkle,* **MOKSHA**

4

5

1

2

3

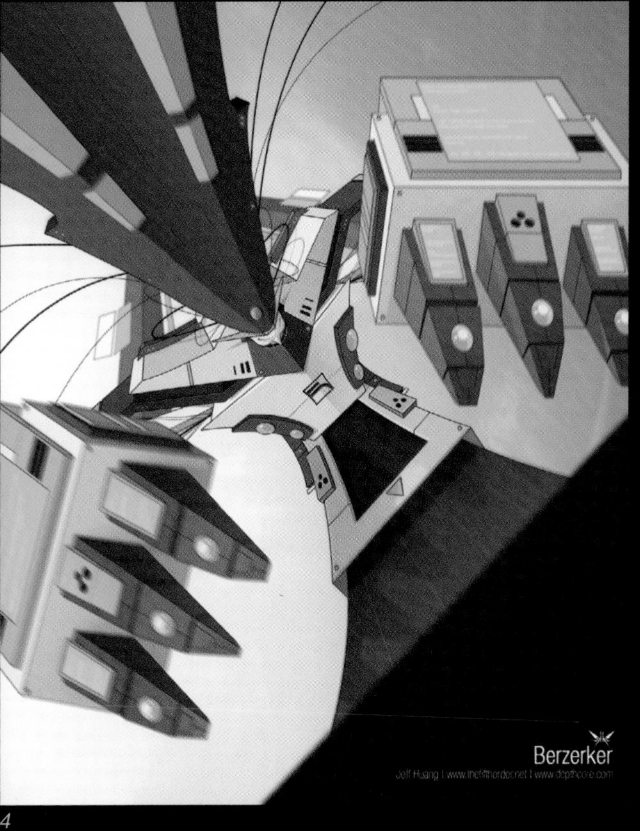

4

1. *Ari Weinkle,* **SUNLIT**
2. *Ari Weinkle,* **RHINESTONES AND MORALS**
3. *Feliz Ajenjo,* **INTERACTIVE COFFEE**
4. *Jeff Huang,* **BERZERKER**
5. *Ari Weinkle,* **THE BLIZZARD, THE DREAMWEAVER**

5

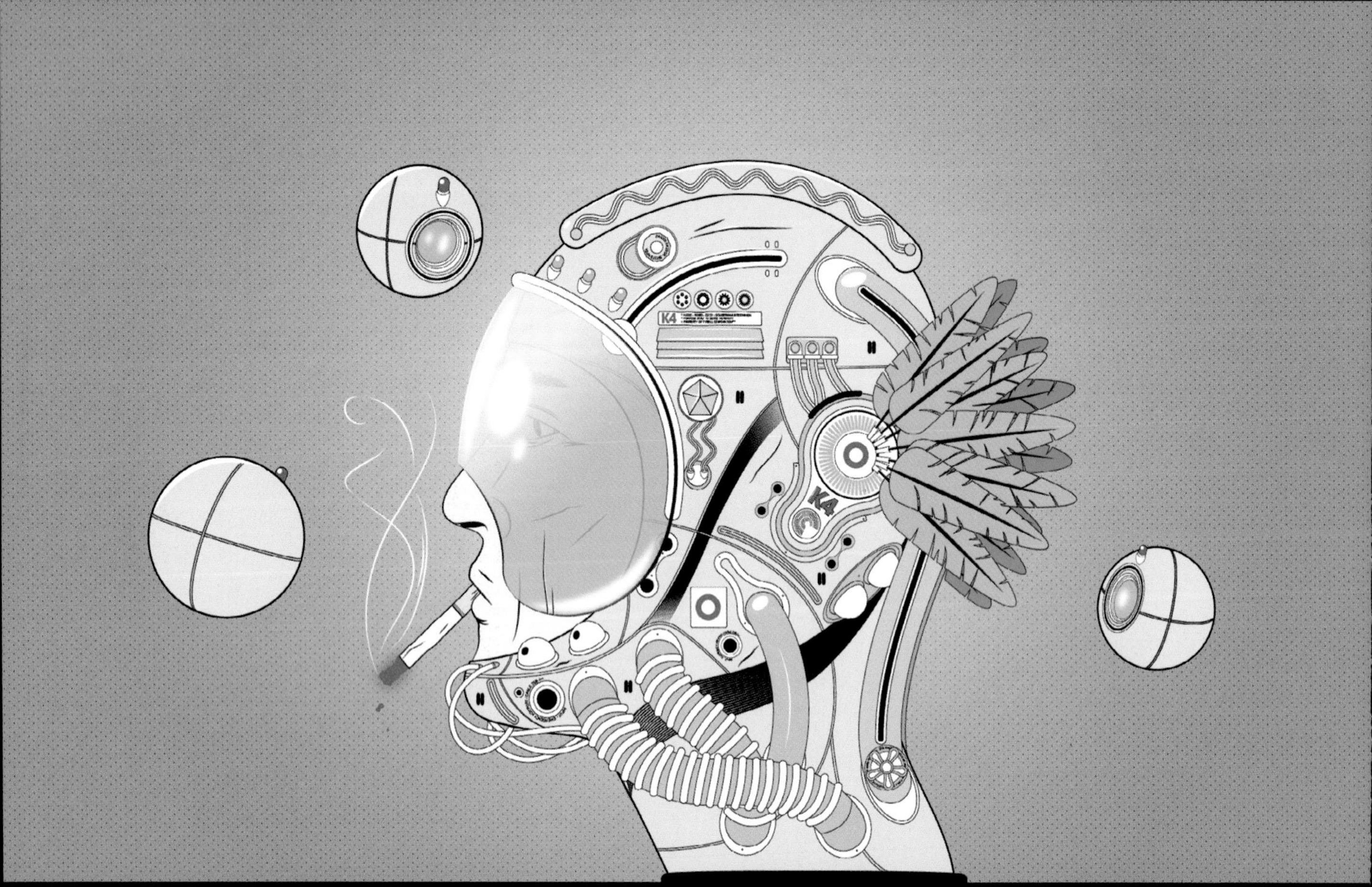

1

1. *Karan Singh,* K4000
2. *Karan Singh,* A DOG'S BREAKFAST
3. *Ollip-ekka Auhlainen,* LE GRAND CIRQUE DES COULEURS
4. *Karan Singh,* RACHEL
5. *Jeff Huang,* BUBBLELICIOUS
6. *Karan Singh,* EDGE OF DESIRE

2

3

4

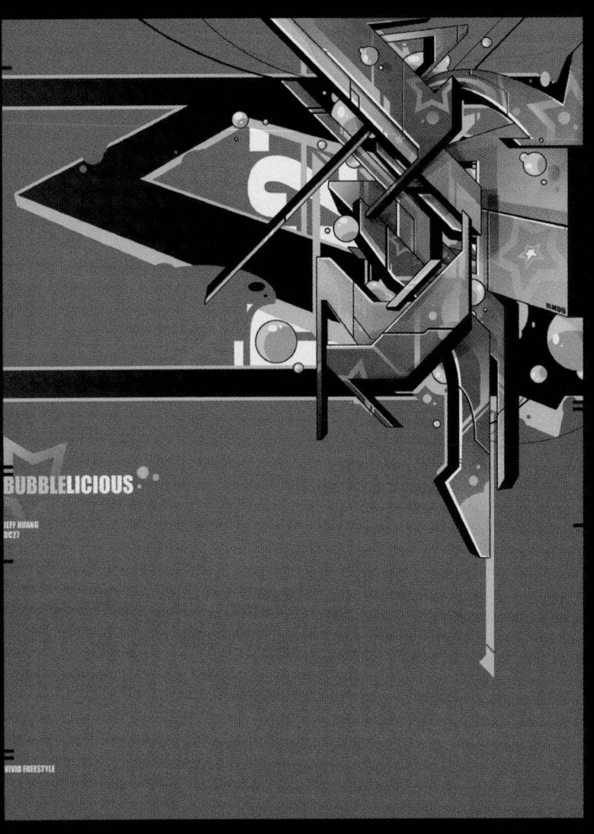

5

6

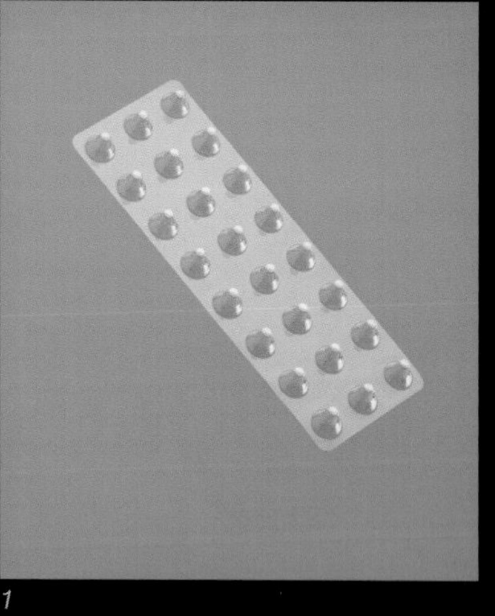

1

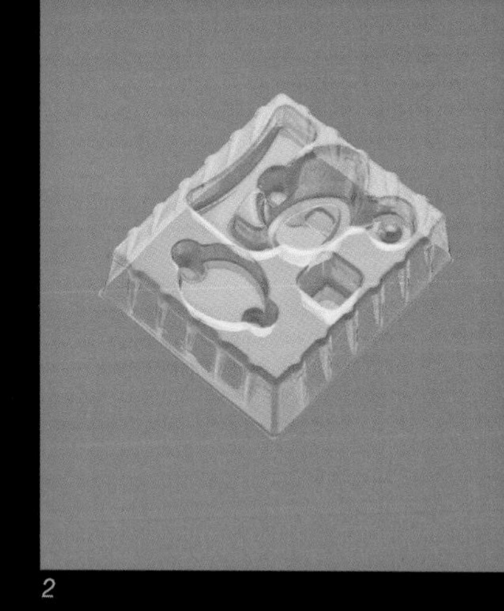

2

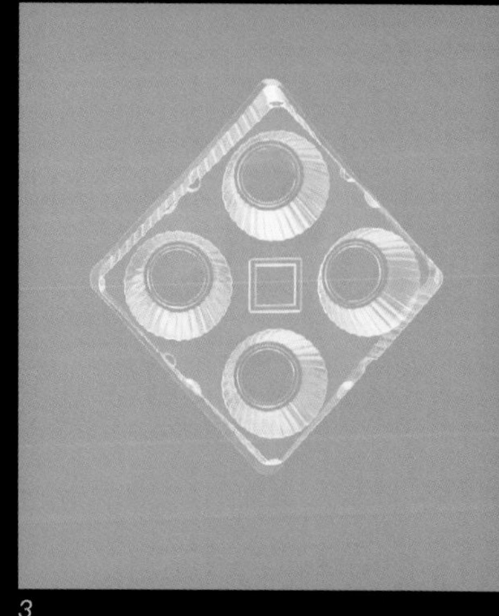

3

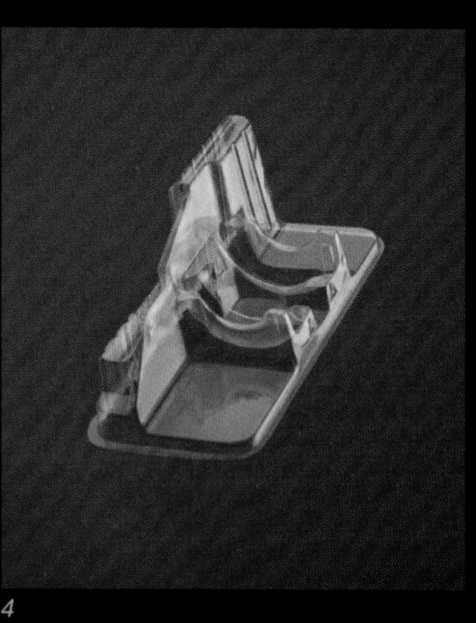

4

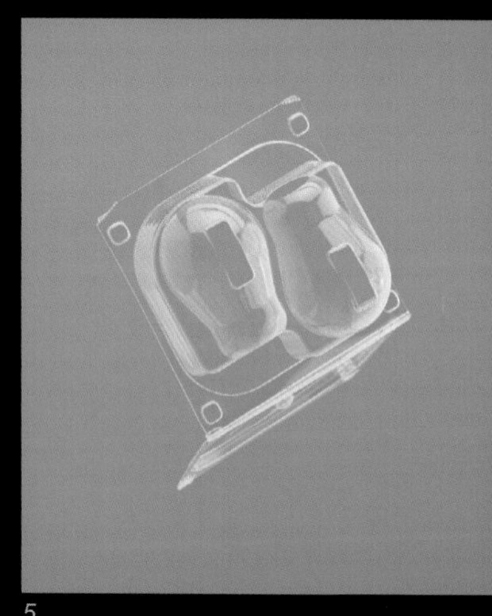

5

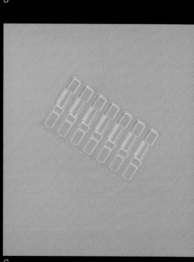

6

1. *Simon Duhamel,* CHOCOLATE BOTTLES
2. *Simon Duhamel,* COLORIMETER ORANGE (V2)
3. *Simon Duhamel,* DESSERT CUPS PINK
4. *Simon Duhamel,* DOORKNOB WOOD
5. *Simon Duhamel,* LIGHT BULB GREEN
6. *Simon Duhamel,* SYRINGES
7. *Simon Duhamel,* SPEAKERS RED

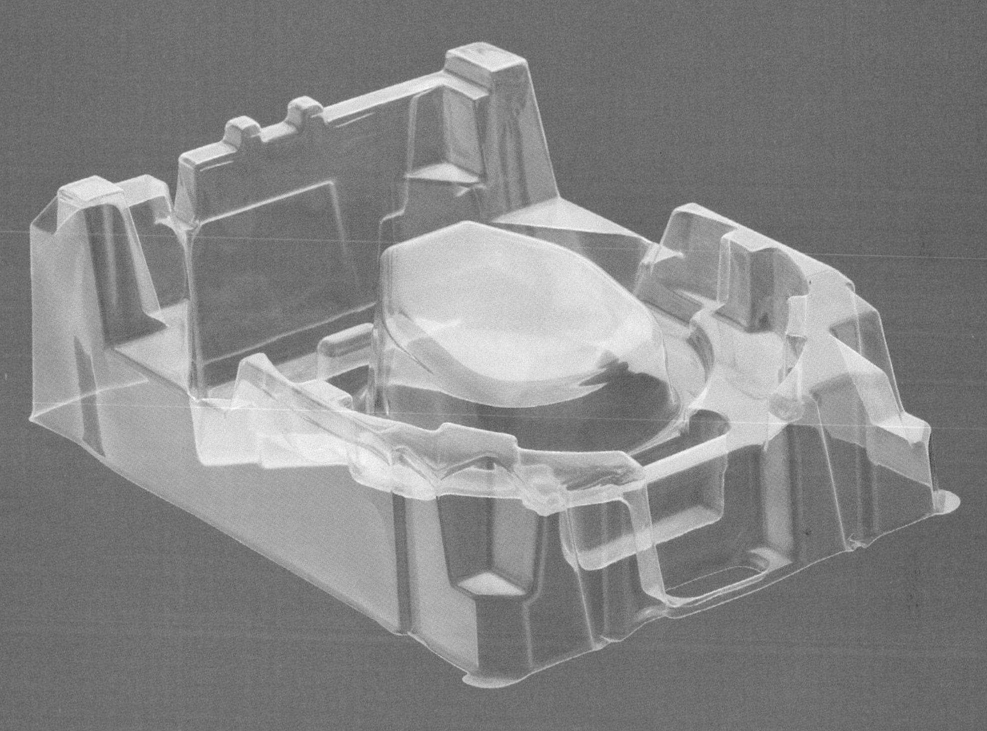

Interview

Cristiano Siqueira

Brazilian illustrator Cristiano Siqueira, aka CrisVector (www.crisvector.com), recounts his own vector art success story as follows: "After getting a technical degree in communication design, I started working with graphic design in books, magazines, and CD covers. Some years later I went into packaging design for the food and toy industry. With such experience, I finally felt comfortable working by myself as a freelance artist, but I chose to work with illustrations, an old passion and my real skill. Since 2005, I've been a full-time illustrator, working from my own small 'home' office, focusing on packaging and graphic design, publishing, advertising, and everything that needs to be illustrated." Cristiano is also the author of the tutorial that follows this interview.

How did you start your career as a digital artist? Did you always know that you wanted to be a designer?

I started my career in a way that's typical of Brazilian designers: as a trainee, doing small jobs in a graphic design studio, working as an assistant to the assistant, cutting off backgrounds of photos, redrawing logos. In other words, learning the basics by doing basic work.

I always wanted to create images, but early on, I didn't realize that I could make a career of it. I started my studies by trying to learn more about techniques of drawing and painting. At that time, I wanted to be a comic artist, but at the end of the course, I had learned a bit more about the design industry and how it works and I became very interested in the illustration field. I was ready to work as an illustrator, but I didn't find many opportunities in that field at that time, so I started with graphic design.

How did you develop your style, and what made you explore it further? What, in your opinion, is its defining characteristic?

Finding a good style can be challenging. I didn't know I had a style before people started telling me I did. In the design industry, artists usually need to be able to work in different styles if they don't want to be restricted to few clients. That was the case with me. I learned to work in different styles in order to be able to meet as many client requests as possible, and I never thought about having a "personal" style. I didn't know it was important.

After spending time working as an illustrator, on my own I started to explore older works, such as old comic pages. I completed sketchbooks; did work for friends, girlfriends, and family; and did experimental exercises, trying to develop a personal style and find my identity as an artist. From studying older works I discovered that they were very close to the comic book style, and that was what I really loved to do. By coincidence (or synchronicity), at the same time I was working on a potential comic book project called *Daniel Dume*, and I thought, "Why did I stop doing that?" Then I started to work in comics again, trying to develop my personal style.

I'm still improving it, creating a solid style library of resources to answer all requests, to be able to use this style commercially too, even though I developed the style for personal reasons.

The defining characteristic of my style is the line, how I use lines to give feeling of depth and shading, movement. Another characteristic is the comic book-derived style, using bright colors and simple shading. Lately, I've been doing many illustrations for magazines and portraits, and I see that this style suits these publications well—and this makes me happy.

How would you describe the workflow for your projects? How would you break it down into steps?

I have some well-defined workflow steps that I follow, and they don't change much between commercial or personal projects. The only difference is that on commercial works, I get the brief from the client, and with personal projects, I give the brief to myself.

With commercial projects, I get the brief, read it, and start thinking about different ways to represent the idea, concept, or subject in an illustration. If I am struggling with the concept, I try to find references that are relevant to what I'm working on. These references don't need to be ready concepts or illustrations on the theme, but information, research, and opinions on the subject, as well as movies or music that relate to it. What I try to discover is how people think about such subjects to be able to create relevant work.

Then, with an idea in mind, I start to create small sketches using a tablet and Photoshop or even a pencil and paper. These sketches are like thumbnails, where I can define the main characteristics of the illustration, the placement of the objects, and the overall composition. Usually, I do three or more different versions and I consider the best two. When I'm working on a client piece, I can send them different versions if they request it.

As soon as I have a sketch approved, I start to give more substance to the sketch, providing detail about the objects. At this point in the process, I work in the size of the final work but still in low resolution (100 or 150dpi). Also at this time, I find lots of references for all the objects that I need to draw. It's impossible to remember all the details of objects, so the references are really useful.

Also, I like to check anatomy in photos to make sure it's correct in my work. I love to draw people and I've done it for many years, but I still don't feel safe drawing everything by memory.

Finally, with the detailed sketch done (often with colors included), I finish the drawing in Illustrator, using a Wacom tablet and Illustrator custom brushes to draw all the lines, as well as other details, shading, and all elements. After this step, I complete the rendering with colors and subtle shading with two or three shading layers and some points of light. After I'm finished, I export the work to a PSD (Photoshop) file, check and correct the colors in Photoshop, and deliver it to the client.

What's the role of the computer in your creative process?

The computer is a great tool—that's all. It's just one of many resources that make the process of "putting ideas out" easier. I try to use the computer as much I can. Nowadays, I do 100 percent of my work on a computer. This is not so much a conceptual choice as a practical one, because I don't have a space to paint and I can't do my work fast enough if I use paper. The creative approach is still the same, whether on computer or paper, but I always finish my projects on a computer.

Could you list some artists and designers you admire?

I like the Brazilian comic artists Fábio Moon and Gabriel Bá, not just for their great work but for their honesty in talking about all the aspects of their work, both good and bad things. Many times, I've heard them speak about their work, and I learn something every time. It's inspiring to know that some people can be great without betraying their principles.

I love J.C. Leyendecker's work as well. My dream is to be at least 30 percent as good as he was.

Tell us about some of your own works that you are proudest of, and explain why they are so important to you.

I can tell you about some recent works that I did when I decided to get back to my old style. Their significance is related not just to the result, but to the good feeling of finally meeting myself in my works. I was happy to get an opportunity to create some of these works for clients too.

Apart from the money you make, what satisfaction do you get from your work? And how much does this matter in your life?

I like the communication aspect of the work I do. This is what makes me more passionate about illustration, to be able to communicate concepts and ideas without language barriers. When I'm working, I feel like talking with many people, getting them to listen to what I say, getting them thinking and exploring their own thoughts about a subject. Communication is the key for civilization to foster good understanding among different people, and I'm proud to make a small contribution to this with my work.

What advice do you have for those who are starting out their career? What kinds of references are important for those who want to work with this style?

Here's my advice: Find out everything you can about the field in which you want to work. It's important to know how people work and what they need, as well as learn about standard pricing, contracts, and such.

Don't be shy about showing your work, but make sure you show relevant work to prospective clients. It doesn't make sense to show illustrations of fruit to the editor of a magazine who uses only portraits. It's good to be able to create all kinds of work and use it in the right place.

As for sources on style, I suggest that readers take a look at all references possible, including movies, books, comics, and artbooks. It's important to follow what's happening in the market, so it's a good exercise to look at other artists' portfolios, galleries, and websites. The key is not to copy a style, but to know what other people have done and create a new style for yourself.

Tutorial

Technical Vector Illustration by Cristiano Siquiera

In this tutorial, I explain how I created a technical vector illustration I used in a picture I did recently for *ESPN The Magazine*. It features the late Brazilian race car driver and legend Ayrton Senna. For me, it was an honor and a pleasure to have the opportunity to create that picture.

Step 1

My work always begins with finding references. I don't feel safe just drawing from memory. I need to see the details of what I'm drawing; I need to see variations of light and angles, and have a better idea of the object that I'm representing.

Ordinarily, to create a portrait of Ayrton Senna, I would get Ayrton to pose for a round of sketches, which would be impossible for obvious reasons. The solution was to observe some pictures, and because the work was commissioned by *ESPN The Magazine*, I asked their staff to send some pictures (**1**). I also sought other pictures so I could get a better sense of depth and feel confident when shading the image.

Step 2

Even with the references, you need to do a sketch for the client to approve. At this stage, I also take this opportunity to plan the illustration graphically, considering the styles, points of light, framing, and elements that will comprise the final work. In this case, the client requested that I base the illustration on one particular photo, but I used several others as references, too, so I could apply the details of expression and light variations (**2**).

1

2

Step 3

With the sketch approved, I completed the illustration using Adobe Illustrator. I placed the sketch in one layer (with Opacity set at 30%) and all the references in another layer. Then I created two more layers: one for the traits and another for the colors (**3**).

Step 4

One of the things I discovered not long ago with Illustrator is the advantage of using the brushes along with a tablet. Since I discovered this, my job has totally changed. I started using Illustrator to create the organic look I always wanted for my work.

In Illustrator, I work with a set of three custom brushes. Customizing a brush in Illustrator is simple: Open the Brushes menu by selecting Window > Brushes. You will see a series of custom brushes. Double-click any of the Calligraphic brushes, and a screen will appear with several options. Name your new brush, set the angle, choose whether it will be fixed or variable with respect to tablet pressure, and set the angle of variation. The same goes for the other options: Roundness and Diameter. When choosing settings for these last two options, always specify the "pressure" to be able to take full advantage of the tablet (**4**).

3

4

Step 5

In the selected layer, choose settings that will give style to your work. In this example, below the selected layer I have the sketch layer, set at 30% Opacity, that will guide me in the drawing (**5**). The drawing step is usually the one that takes the most time and effort; it's here that I handle all the detail, shading, textures, expressions, and black areas, if there are any. At this stage, I work with the tablet almost exclusively, hardly ever using the mouse. I do all my tracing with the Brush tool and, in black areas, with the Pencil tool.

In smaller areas, I use a thinner brush, and in larger areas I use a thicker one. When in doubt as to the form of the subject's face, I usually work with reference photos around so that I can observe the face from different angles and different lighting.

Shading can be done in countless ways. My approach follows a style borrowed from the techniques of ink drawing and comics, with hatches and variation in line thickness. Every illustrator needs to develop an approach that's suitable to his or her style.

5

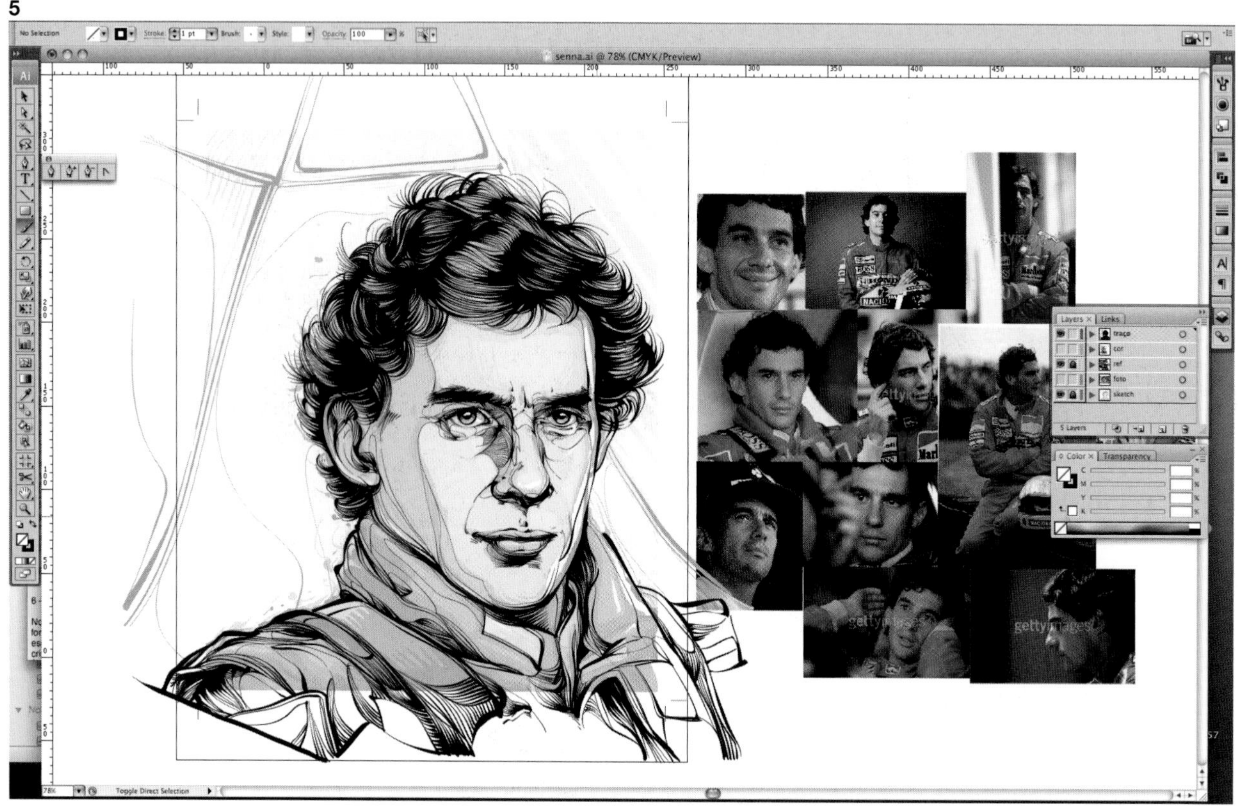

Step 6

In my work, colors serve a complementary function. I use between one and three steps of color, like a kind of cell shading. Try using bright colors to contrast with the dark lines and create a more vibrant look for the final work.

Sometimes, I need to create extra volume areas, besides the three steps, so I can make the illustration more like the reference. Some people have unique nuances in the skin that need to be represented in illustrations. With the Ayrton illustration, fortunately, I was able to reproduce many of the details and not depend on the traits of both colors (**6**).

6

Step 7

When I finish work in Illustrator, I always export a TIF file at 300dpi to make minor color adjustments in Photoshop if necessary (**7**).

Conclusion

Compare your work to the completed image on the following page. If it looks similar, and you're satisfied with what you see, your work is done.

7

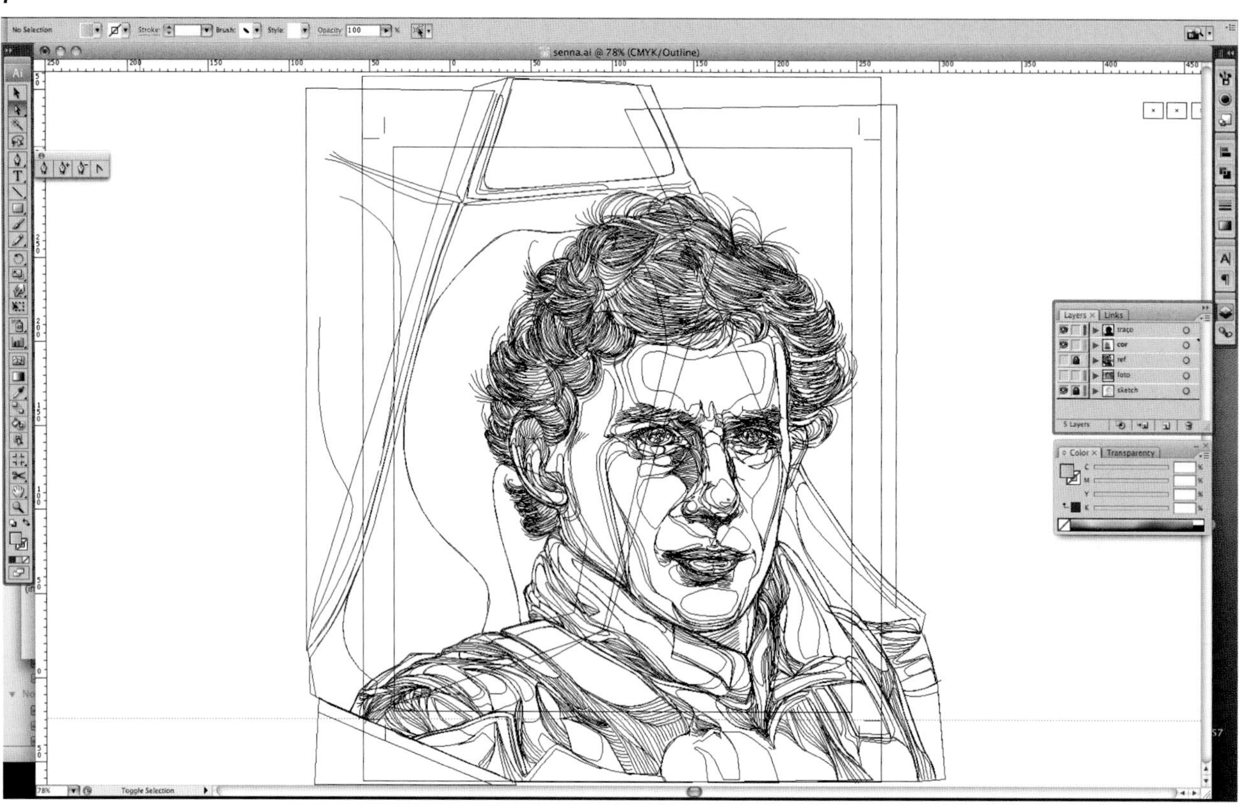

CHAPTER 7

NEOSURREALISM

Neosurrealism is an art genre born out of the old Surrealism movement and its rich and varied ways of expression. Surrealism was a cultural movement put together by a group of writers and visual artists in the early 1920s, led by André Breton, who considered Surrealism, above all, to be a revolutionary movement within the art world.

The philosophy behind the Surrealist movement was to react against what its members saw as the destruction wrought by the "rationalism" guiding European culture toward the horrors of World War II.

Surrealism also provided a means of reuniting conscious and unconscious realms of experience so completely that the world of dream and fantasy would be joined to the everyday rational world in "an absolute reality, a surreality."

STEAMPUNK ICECREAM,
by Aiven

A lot of great artists joined the movement, such as Giorgio de Chirico, Max Ernst, Joan Miró, Francis Picabia, Yves Tanguy, and Salvador Dalí, along many others.

Throughout the 1930s Surrealism enjoyed its golden age, and as a visual movement, it sought to expose psychological truth by stripping ordinary objects of their normal meaning in order to create compelling images that existed beyond ordinary, formal organization, and thus evoke empathy from the viewer.

1. *Jeff Huang,* AISLES OF TRANCE
2. *Benjamin Low,* REACH FOR THE SKY

1

The movement continued and met with great recognition over the years. By the late 1970s, surrealism had evolved into an artistic genre that illustrates the complex imagery of dream or subconscious visions in irrational space and forms of combinations, a style now known as Neosurrealism.

Neosurrealism, which is sometimes called Modern Surrealism, does not embrace the original surrealist idea of a freedom from rational control. But it's unmistakably a thriving artistic genre that was inspired by the old Surrealism movement.

1. *Felix Ajenjo,* EXTRACTION
2. *Jeff Huang,* COMCAST GO—SANDAL ENVY
3. *Jeff Huang,* DIARY
4. *Jeff Huang,* COMCAST GO—FUN IN THE PARK

3

1

Technology has opened up great new vistas for art and the ways we can visually communicate. The old computer-generated visual media are now part of digital art, which is considered one of the most commonly used media in the creation of Neosurrealist pieces.

Today, we have many great artists keeping Neosurrealism alive, depicting the imagery of dreams and the subconscious mind and intriguing many viewers all over the globe.

1. *Mart Biemans,* **THE INFINITE WORLD**
2. *Jeff Huang,* **MEMOIR**

1. *Sorin Bechira,* THE KING'S BURDEN
2. *Przemek Nawrocki,* MEDUSA
3. *Sorin Bechira,* THERE'S NO REASON TO BE SAD

1

2

Interview

Nik Ainley

Nik Ainley is a UK-based digital artist who taught himself Photoshop while studying physics at London's Imperial College. He produces both personal and commissioned digital art, and his works have appeared in various digital art magazines. His clients have included British Airways, British Film Institute, Adobe, Computer Arts, Nickelodeon, Harper Collins, *National Geographic*, Starbucks, and UNICEF. He works primarily in Photoshop, but his illustrations may also incorporate work done in Cinema 4D and Adobe Illustrator. You can read more about Nik and see more of his work at www.shinybinary.com.

How did you start your career as a digital artist? Did you always know that you wanted to pursue digital art as a career?

I stumbled into digital art purely by accident. I can't remember why I first started playing around with Photoshop, but I do remember being hooked right from the start. Before that, I had played around briefly with programs such as Macromedia Fireworks and Corel Photo-Paint, but they didn't feel right to me the way Photoshop did. It took many years from first trying out Photoshop to becoming a full-time digital illustrator, and I think all the practice I put in helped me hit the ground running as a commercial artist.

When I was younger I thought I would end up as a scientist of some sort. I never really thought I had any artistic talent, and seemed to do far better at math and science at school. Things have turned out very differently from how I imagined.

How did you come up with your style? What made you explore and develop this style, and what, in your opinion, is its defining characteristic?

I don't have any particular aesthetic style that I find most appealing; I like to try everything. As far as I'm concerned, whatever looks good works. I try to make my images have visual impact and use any techniques or styles necessary. I tend to do a fair amount of typographic illustrations. Partly, this is due to demand and to the fact that I can do them. Once I started to have a few type-based images in my portfolio, people would commission me for more and slowly these types of images became the most important part of my work.

How would you describe your workflow for your projects? How would you break it into steps?

My workflow varies depending on what kind of project I'm doing. Sometimes it's 3D-based and will require a lot of work in a 3D app before I head into Photoshop. Other times it might be more photo-based and will start with me spending a huge amount of time browsing photos to find one suitable for the project. Whatever I do to start a project, though, I always end up finishing an image off in Photoshop, and use my standard techniques to add that extra level of shine and detail I like to put in my images.

626
XXX

What's the role of the computer in your creative process?

I am an entirely digital illustrator. Almost without exception, I do everything on my computer. Very occasionally, when I have some tricky shape to do in 3D, I'll scribble down a sketch of what I want to work off, but that's very rare. For me, the software gives me the power and flexibility to help bring the ideas in my head into existence. I could never manage the same with traditional techniques.

Can you list some artists/designers you admire?

There are lots of folks in the Depthcore collective who inspire me consistently. Other than that I browse loads of different stuff; I can't even remember one-tenth of the people whose work I've seen and loved. I do like the artist Jeff Soto a lot, and many artists involved in the visual effects industry—matte painters, concept artists, and so forth.

BIRTHDAY

GO
PLAY

Tell us about some of your works that you are proudest of, and explain why they are so important to you.

I'm proud of two images I did earlier this year called *Julia* and *Origins*, because they both represent a huge amount of time and effort. They are also the first images I have really put more advanced 3D work into, and that could not have been achieved in Photoshop. For me, they are perhaps a glimpse of the future direction my work could head in.

Apart from the money you make, what type of satisfaction do you get from your work? And how much does this matter in your life?

When I'm working on an image and I'm liking what I'm seeing, I'm pretty much at my happiest. I can spend hours tinkering at my computer without even noticing time passing. The satisfaction of finishing an image I like and sitting back to admire lasts a few days.

Unfortunately, after that I tend to get bored with what I've done quite quickly and want to move on to something new. I think it's good not to rest on your laurels, though, and always be looking to the next image. I see my illustrations as stepping-stones on the way to future images that will be closer to what I have in my head.

What advice do you have for those who are starting out in their careers?

Enjoy what you do. Try to do your own thing and not follow other people's trends. Don't get depressed if your work doesn't start out at the best quality; everyone begins like that.

Tutorial

Surreal Composition in Photoshop

Surrealism is one of my favorite art movements because it's much more than a representation of reality; it's an attempt to make subconscious ideas come true in art. If you take a look at some surreal images, you'll notice some patterns like the horizon and skies using a sort of desert/blue color scheme, especially in some Salvador Dalí paintings.

With that in mind, in this tutorial I'll show you how to create a surreal composition in Photoshop. We will basically use a few stock photos and mix them in order to create the surreal style. The process is not difficult, but it is quite long. Be prepared to spend at least two hours looking for images and adjusting colors and details to make your project look cool.

Step 1

To create a surreal image, it's always necessary to start with some sort of desert/dunes image. For this project, I began with a stock photo courtesy of Shutterstock that had a nice color scheme. You can find it at www.shutterstock.com/pic-72629506/stock-photo-sahara-desert-safari-off-road-vehicle-driving-in-the-awbari-sand-sea-libya.html (**1**).

Step 2

The only problem with the image I chose is that it included a car. To get rid of it I selected the Spot Healing Brush tool (J), and for the type of brush I chose Content Aware (**2**). This tool is magical; you simply start painting over the areas you want to remove and Photoshop will do the dirty job of filling those areas with the right content.

Step 3

Keep cleaning the image (**3**).

1

2

3

Step 4

Keep working with the Spot Healing Brush tool (J) (**4**). Almost there.

Step 5

This image shows what your image should look like after using the Spot Healing Brush tool (**5**). As you can see, the result is quite impressive.

Step 6

Create a new document in Photoshop using the Letter format. Then import the dunes photo and place it in the document. You will have to make the sand part a bit bigger, which you can do easily by use the Rectangular Marquee tool (M), and then choosing Edit > Transform > Scale (**6**).

4

5

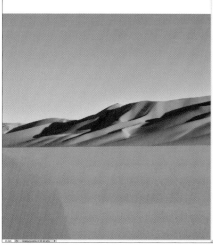

6

Step 7

Now let's add another stock photo. The one shown here comes from Shutterstock and can be found at www.shutterstock.com/pic-46881736/stock-photo-extreme-terrain-sahara-desert.html. Place the new image on top of the original image (**7**).

Step 8

Now we need to get rid of the sky and the dunes. Select the newly imported image on top, and change the Blend Mode setting to Overlay. Also, using the Eraser tool (E), start deleting the image as it gets closer to the horizon (**8**).

Step 9

Choose Layer > New Adjustment Layer > Hue and Saturation. Use –5 for Hue, 48 for Saturation, and –5 for Lightness. Also choose Layer > Create Clipping Mask, and make sure that the adjustment layer is on top of the image you want to apply the effect to (**9**). That way, the adjustment will be applied only on that image and not in the other layers.

7

8

9

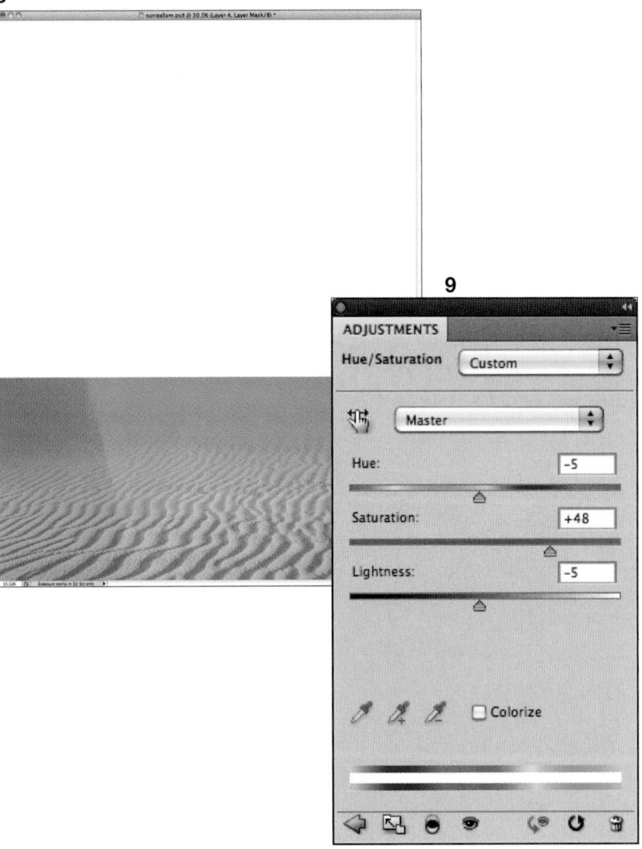

Step 10

Add a new layer beneath the others and fill it with a gradient using shades of blue. The ones I used are #469ccd for the dark blue and #4c9ece for the light one (**10**).

Step 11

On top of the other layers, add another adjustment layer. Choose Layer > New Adjustment Layer > Hue and Saturation. Use 0 for Hue, –28 for Saturation, and –5 for the Lightness (**11**).

Step 12

Return to Layer > New Adjustment Layer > Levels. Use 45 for the Black input, 1 for the Gray input, and 255 for the White input (**12**).

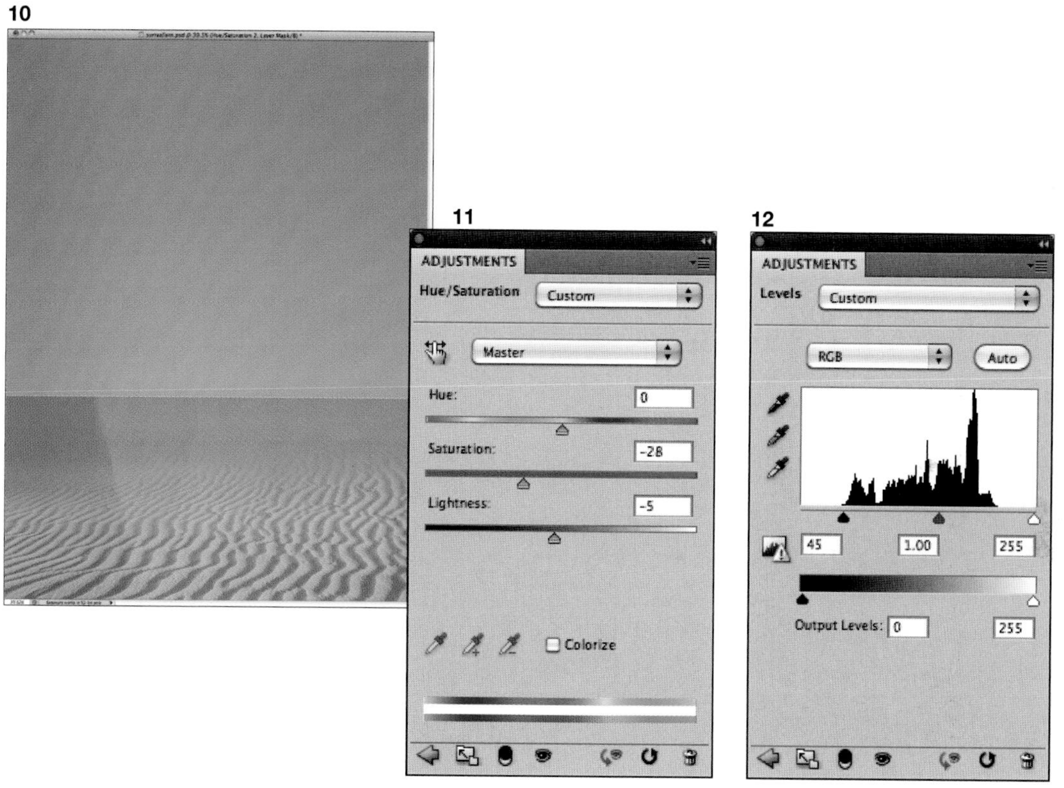

Step 13

Let's add a moon—it's always important to have a moon in the middle of the day in a nice surrealist image. The one you see in this image is from Shutterstock and you can find it here: www.shutterstock.com/pic-40812199/stock-photo-moon.html (**13**).

Step 14

Change the blend mode of the image to Screen in order to make the black transparent (**14**).

Step 15

Now let's make the sky a bit more apocalyptic. As I said in the beginning, this composition is nothing more than a mix of photos. You can find the one I used for this step at www.shutterstock.com/pic-73900090/stock-photo-railway-to-horizon.html. In this image, I just used the sky and placed it in my design. For Blend Mode, use Hard Light (**15**).

Step 16

In Step 15, the horizon didn't look real because the transition wasn't smooth. To smooth the transition, you can use either the Eraser tool or a layer mask to make the sand fade out into the sky (**16**).

13

14

15

16

Step 17

Add a new layer on top of the other layers. Then select the Brush tool (B), and using brown for the color (#a87434), paint the area that goes from the middle of the ground to half of the sky (**17**).

Step 18

Change the blend mode of the brown layer to Hard Light at 60% opacity (**18**).

Step 19

In the image in Step 16, the moon was too bright, so you need to reduce its opacity to 70% (**19**). Now our surrealist environment is practically done. It's time to add some other elements.

17

18

19

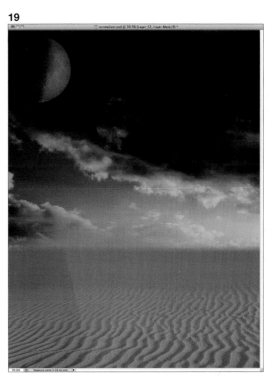

Step 20

Select a photo of a model. You can find the one I used at www.shutterstock.com/pic-73496035/stock-photo-beautiful-female-face-sexy-model-closeup-portrait-isolated-on-white-background-glamour-fashion.html.

Using the Lasso tool (L) or the Pen tool (P), select a part of the model's face only, using this image for reference. Then delete the rest, keeping only the part you selected (**20**).

Step 21

Choose Layer > Layer Style > Inner Shadow. Use Overlay for the Blend Mode setting, 100% for the Opacity value, 120° for Angle, 9 pixels for Distance, 26% for Choke, and 35 pixels for Size (**21**).

20

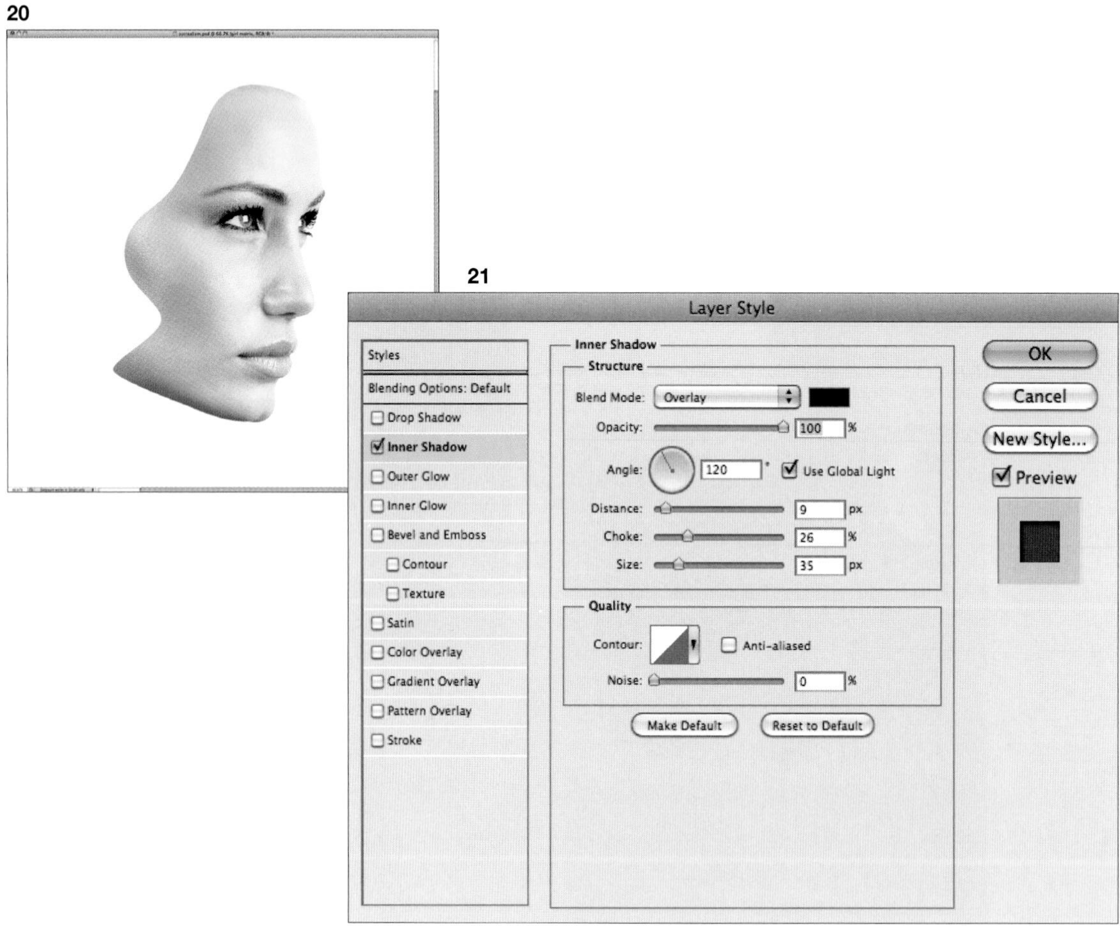

21

Step 22

With these new settings applied, check your image against this one (**22**). Continue to tweak the settings to make sure your image is as close to this one as you can make it.

22

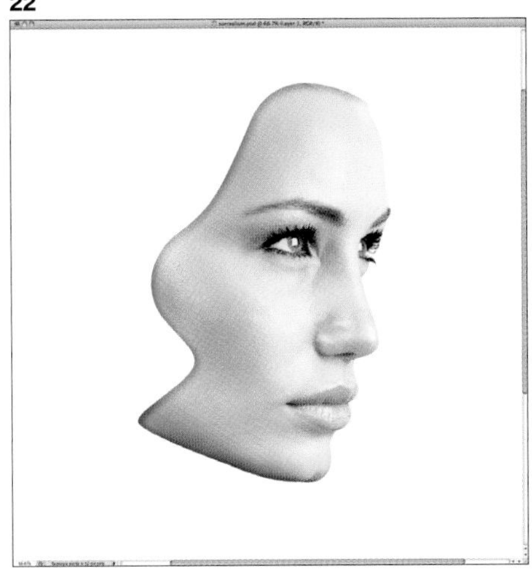

Step 23

Select a skin area and copy, then paste in order to create the back side of the face, as it was just the skin from the rest of the body (**23**).

Step 24

With the Lasso tool (L), select an area that looks more organic. Then mask the skin from the previous step (**24**).

23

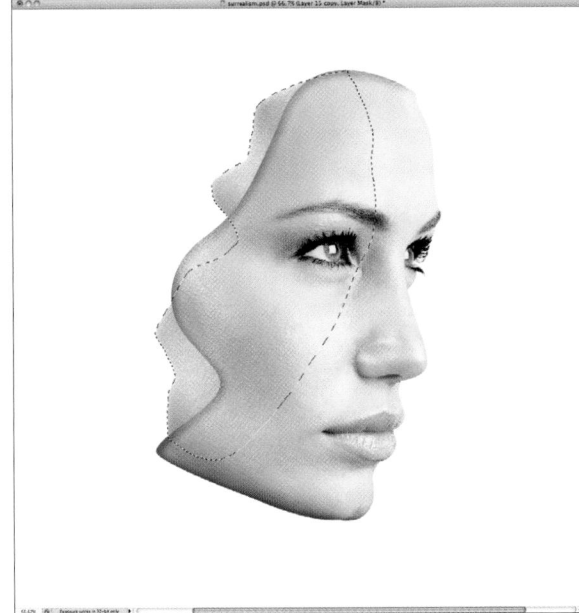

24

Step 25

Duplicate the layer from the previous step and change the Blend Mode setting to Multiply. This part should start to look darker (**25**).

Step 26

Duplicate the layer created in step 24 and choose Image > Adjustment > Desaturate. Then change this layer's Blend Mode to Soft Light. Your result should look like this image (**26**). Now it's time to add this image to your surreal composition.

Step 27

Merge the layers used to assemble the face in a single layer and place it in the composition (**27**).

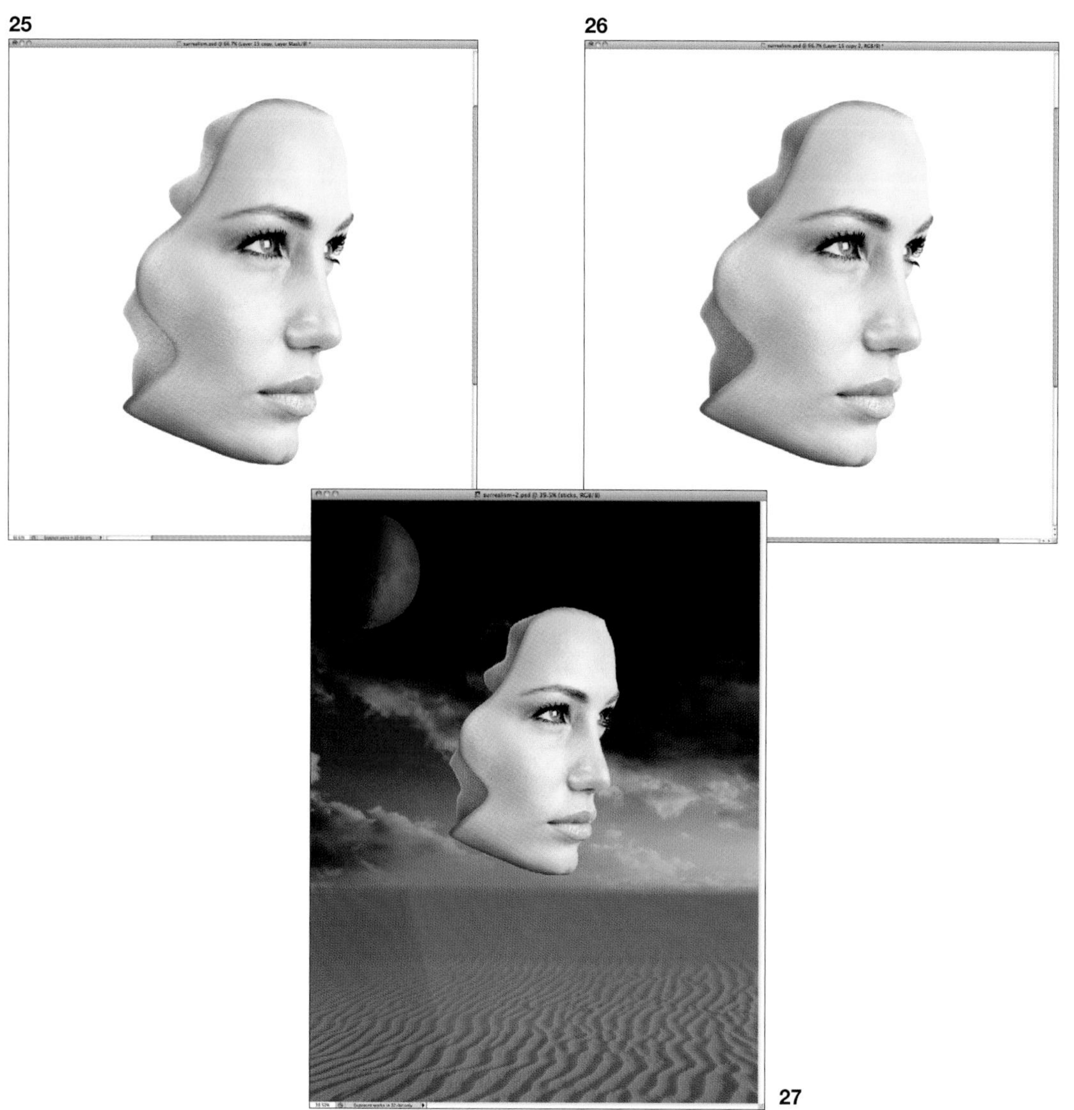

25

26

27

Step 28

Duplicate the face layer and select Image > Adjustment > Desaturate. Then choose Layer > Create Clipping Mask. Change the Blend Mode setting of the layer to Soft Light (**28**).

Step 29

Choose Layer > New Adjustment Layer > Levels. Choose 63 for the Black input, .88 for the Gray input, and 246 for the White input. Then select Layer > Create and create a clipping mask for this layer as well. Now you should have the face layer on top, which is a clipping mask, the black and white layer, and this one (**29**).

Step 30

Return to Layer > New Adjustment Layer > Hue and Saturation to apply more settings. Choose 0 for Hue, –61 for Saturation, and 0 for Lightness (**30**).

28 **29** **30**

Step 31

Compare your results to this image (**31**). This is what you should see after the adjustments made in steps 27–30.

Step 32

Add a new layer on top of the others and then, with the Brush tool (B) and a small rounded brush, create some lines that look like sticks holding the face up in the air. Notice that two of the sticks shown in this image go in front of the face with the other two behind it (**32**).

Step 33

Select the sticks layer you just created and choose Layer > Layer Style > Pattern Overlay. For Pattern, choose Fiber (**33**).

31

32

33

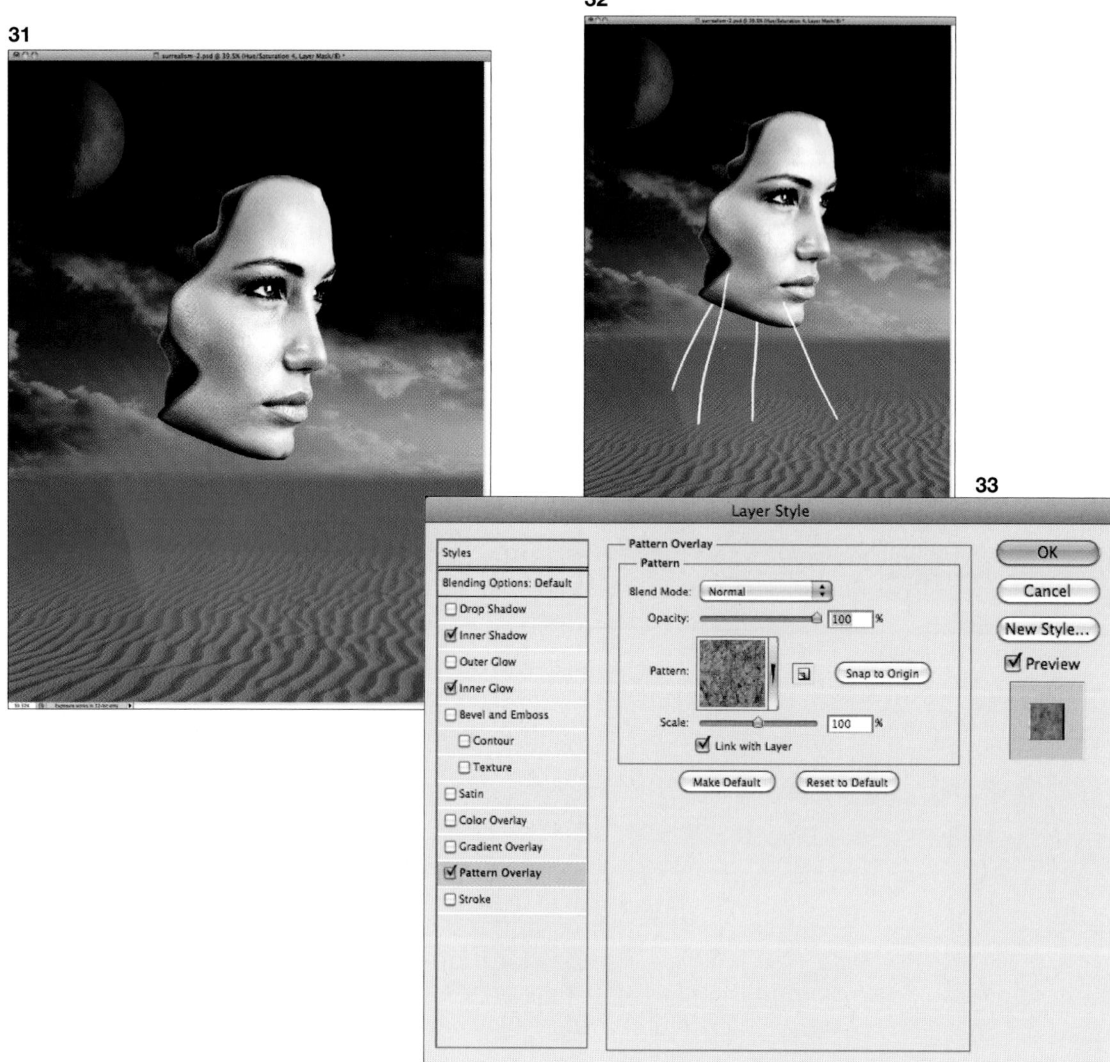

Step 34

Select Inner Glow and apply the following settings: Color Dodge for Blend Mode, 75% for Opacity, 0 for Noise, Edge for Source, 0 for Choke, and 7 pixels for Size (**34**).

Step 35

The last style you choose will be Inner Shadow. Set Color to black, Blend Mode to Darken, Opacity to 84%, Distance to 5 pixels, Choke to 0%, and Size to 9 pixels (**35**).

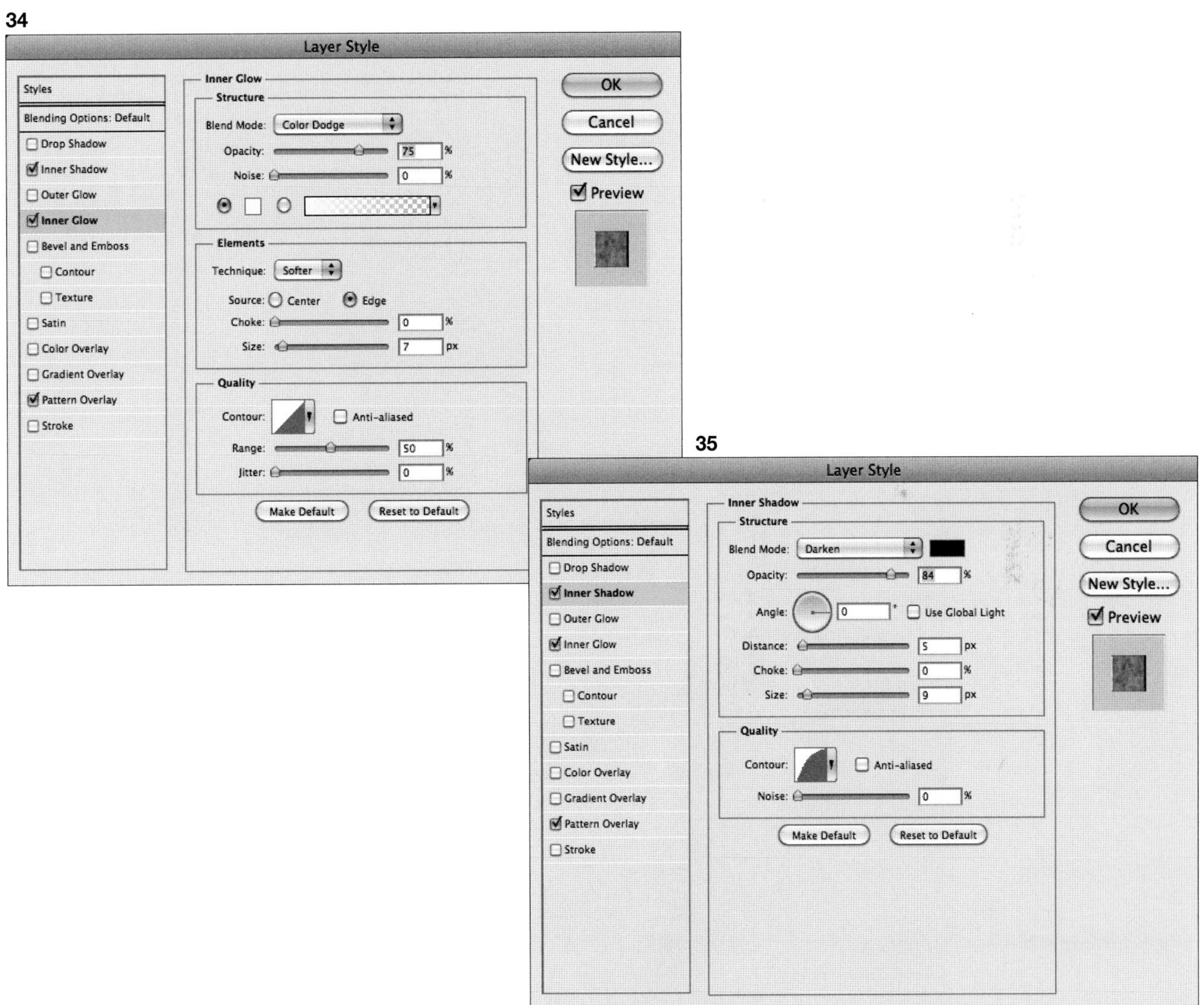

Step 36

Here is the result after the layer styles. Note that the sticks look more real (**36**).

Step 37

With the Brush tool (B) use a very soft brush and create some shadows for the sticks that are in front of the face (**37**).

Step 38

Group this layer in a folder and change the blend mode of the folder to Color Burn (**38**).

36

37

38

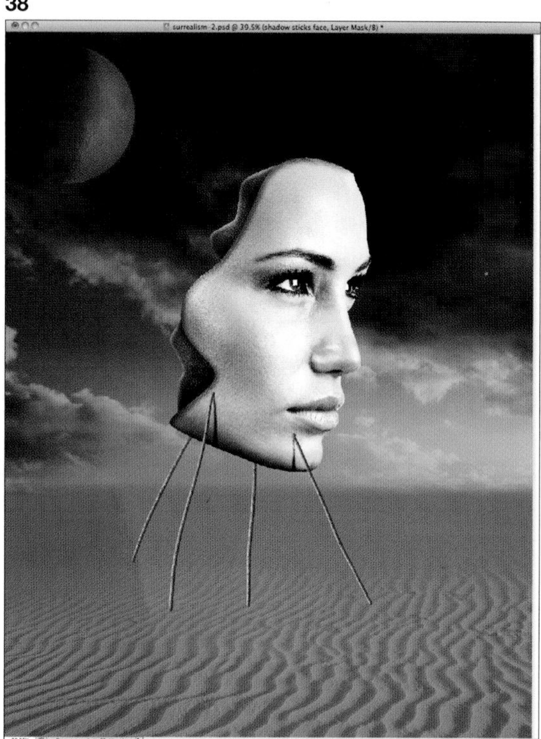

Step 39

Add another layer inside the Color Burn folder and create some shadows where the sticks touch the ground (**39**).

Step 40

With the Brush tool (B) still selected, choose a very soft brush and create a shadow shape for the face and also for the sticks, similar to the one shown in this image. Paint the lips in black by changing Opacity to 30% (**40**).

Step 41

Select all layers used to create the face/sticks and group them in a new folder. Duplicate this folder and merge the group into a layer. Resize it and select Filter > Blur > Gaussian Blur. Use 5 pixels for the Radius setting. Duplicate it again and resize it so you have three faces. Use this image for reference (**41**).

39

40

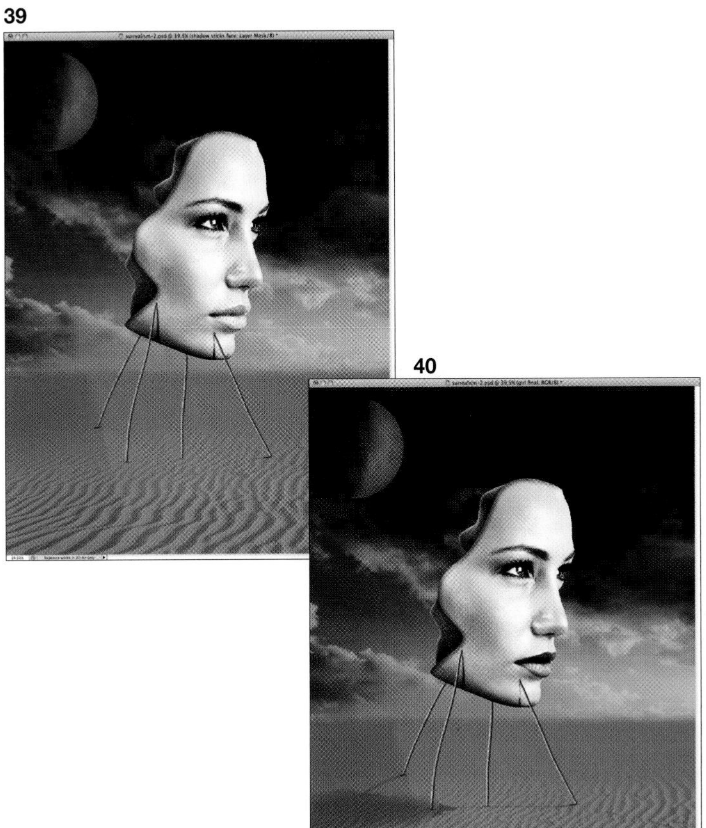

41

Step 42

It wouldn't be a surreal image if it didn't have a person walking toward the horizon. To add that crucial element, I went a little bit further and used an image of a scientist walking in a chemical protection suit. You can find the image I used at www.shutterstock.com/pic-66287641/stock-photo-the-scientific-ecologist-in-overalls-leaves-afar.html.

Extract the scientist from the background and place the figure in the surreal composition. Then select Image > Adjustment > Desaturate, and after that go to Image > Adjustment > Levels. Increase the black input and also reduce the white output to reduce the contrast (**42**).

Step 43

Add a new layer. Choose the Brush tool (B) and select black as the color; then create a shadow for the scientist at 50% Opacity (**43**).

Step 44

Choose Layer > New Adjustment Layer > Hue and Saturation. Make sure this adjustment layer is positioned on top of all the other layers. Then choose 0 for Hue, –20 for Saturation, and +6 for Lightness (**44**).

42

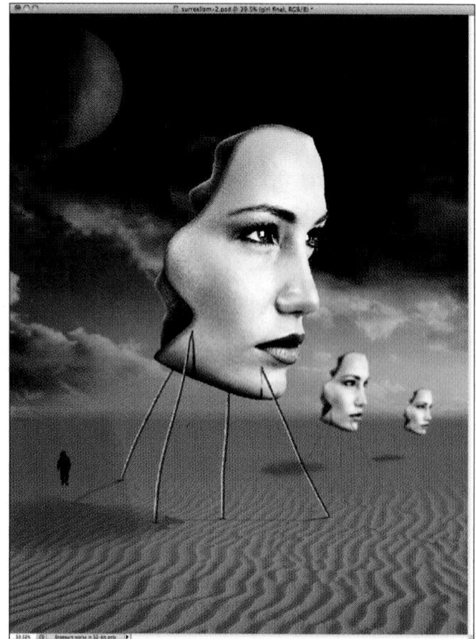

43

44

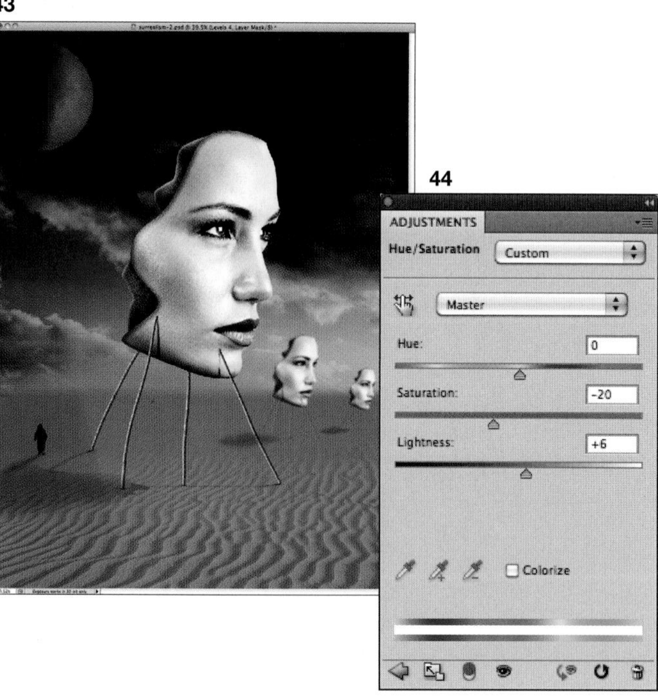

Step 45

Add a new layer on top of the others and fill it with black. Then, using the Brush tool (B) and a very soft brush (and also the biggest brush you can get), paint an ellipse in white. Change the Blend Mode setting of this layer to Linear Blur and Opacity to 30% (**45**).

Step 46

Select all the layers and duplicate them. Merge the duplicated copies into a single layer and select Filter > Noise > Add Noise. Use 1.5% for the Amount value and Gaussian for Distribution (**46**).

Conclusion

Although this tutorial is quite long, the process and techniques involved in compositing an image like the one you just created are quite simple. The most important thing to do when working in a surreal style is to start with a clear idea of what you want to do, then find the right images to realize your idea. The cool thing about this style is that it's very abstract. Because the point of surrealism is to represent your subconscious, rather than some objective reality, everything you do might be correct, as long as you're able to create the image you see in your mind.

45

46

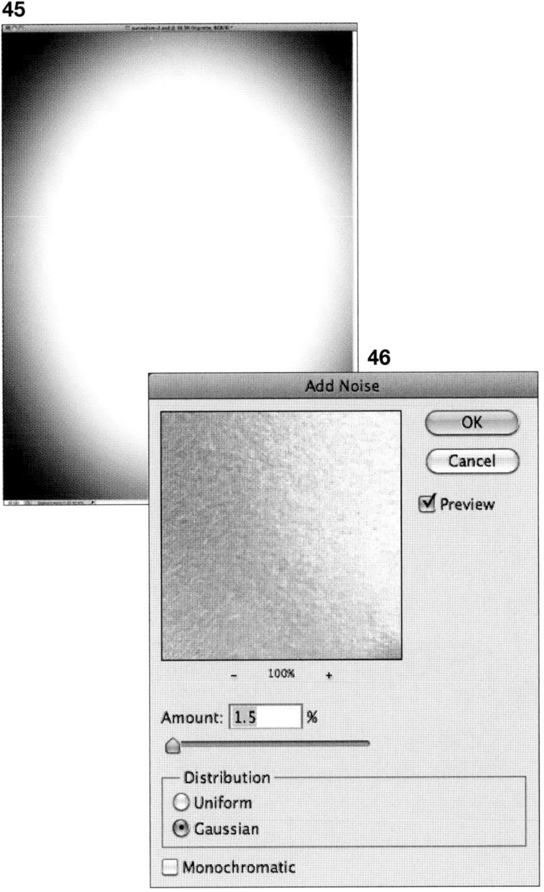

47

Featured Artists

Index

K

L

M

N

O

P

R

S

T

V

W